Learning Technology

FURTHER
EDUCATION

YOU MIGHT ALSO LIKE

The A-Z Guide to Working in Further Education
978-1-909330-85-6
Jonathan Gravells and Susan Wallace

Becoming an Outstanding Personal Tutor: Supporting Learners through Personal Tutoring and Coaching
978-1-910391-05-1
Andrew Stork and Ben Walker

Embedding English and Maths: Practical Strategies for FE and Post-16 Tutors
978-1-910391-70-9
Terry Sharrock

Most of our titles are also available in a range of electronic formats. To order please go to our website www.criticalpublishing.com or contact our distributor, NBN International, 10 Thornbury Road, Plymouth PL6 7PP, telephone 01752 202301 or email orders@nbninternational.com.

Learning Technology

A Handbook for FE Teachers and Assessors

DANIEL SCOTT

FURTHER EDUCATION

First published in 2018 by Critical Publishing Ltd

The author has made every effort to ensure the accuracy of information contained in this publication, but assumes no responsibility for any errors, inaccuracies, inconsistencies and omissions. Likewise, every effort has been made to contact copyright holders. If any copyright material has been reproduced unwittingly and without permission the Publisher will gladly receive information enabling them to rectify any error or omission in subsequent editions.

British Library Cataloguing in Publication Data
A CIP record for this book is available from the British Library

ISBN: 978-1-912096-93-0

This book is also available in the following e-book formats:

MOBI ISBN: 978-1-912096-92-3
EPUB ISBN: 978-1-912096-91-6
Adobe e-book ISBN: 978-1-912096-90-9

The right of Daniel Scott to be identified as the Author of this work has been asserted by him in accordance with the Copyright, Design and Patents Act 1988.

Cover design by Out of House Limited
Text design by Out of House Limited
Project Management by Out of House Publishing Solutions
Printed and bound in Great Britain by 4edge, Essex

Critical Publishing
3 Connaught Road
St Albans
AL3 5RX

www.criticalpublishing.com

Paper from responsible sources

Contents

Meet the author

Daniel Scott

Daniel Scott is a digital learning specialist who began his learning technology career at a further education (FE) college. He proactively developed the effective use of information learning technology (ILT) and eLearning design in learning, teaching and assessment and he specialises in evaluating and developing learning technology tools and designing eLearning resources.

Daniel has been a Certified Member of the Association for Learning Technology (ALT) since 2013 and won the ALT Learning Technologist of the Year award 2016. He holds a Technology Enhanced Learning MSc and is a qualified teacher, assessor and lead internal verifier.

He frequently posts on his professional and personal blog (http://danielscott86.blogspot.com), which includes learning technology and eLearning practices, ideas and challenges with learning.

Acknowledgements

I would like to say a big thank you to those who reviewed the chapters of this book:

» Geoff Rebbeck – eLearning Adviser

» Rachel Evans – Digital Practice Adviser, Nottingham Trent University

Thank you to Darren Purdy who drew the illustrations and Gary Purdy who designed the promotional graphics. You all gave up your busy schedules to help make this publication as useful and appealing as it can be. Your input was valuable and greatly appreciated.

A special thank you to Critical Publishing Ltd, my publisher, and Out of House, my editors, who helped ensure that this text was of a high standard. Also Ann Gravells whose work inspired me to write in a similar accessible style to hers and was encouraging of me writing this. Finally, thanks to the Association for Learning Technology, Jisc and the wider learning technology communities that support this book.

In particular, thanks to Jisc for their kind permission to use the material reproduced in Appendix 1.1 and Appendix 1.2.

Daniel Scott

"*It depends on how much you want something that determines the effort you put in.*"

(Daniel Scott, 2018)

Foreword

Teaching and learning through digital technology is a fascinating subject. The interaction of people with wider life activities administered through digital technology has made the ability to be confident in its use an important life skill, and it is arguably a problem for those that never have the chance. Consequently, it isn't just about the advantages to learning that teachers use digital technology but it is part of the wider training for life that makes using ILT for teachers an essential skill. It ranks in importance with literacy and numeracy.

We have one further challenge as teachers in that we have to deal with digital technology as it presents itself to us rather than something to be managed in an orderly and progressive manner. What makes this so fascinating is that the speed at which digital technology offers options is always faster than our ability to assimilate it, meaning that ILT is always seen as a cutting-edge 'helter skelter' area of developing teacher practice. It provides us with a smorgasbord of opportunities to try different things. This is not a self-managed development but a constant confrontation of the 'new', meaning for teachers it is as much about confidence to explore as it is acquiring the skills to know how to bend, manipulate, adapt and revise software in order to fit it for the best teaching and learning. Teachers then need to know how to redesign learning in order to improve the learner and learning experience. These are important and critical skills for all teachers, and those unable to do this may be overtaken by those teachers that can.

In this book, Daniel provides a grounding in the basics of how to use digital technology in effective teaching and learning. Reminding us that firstly the digital technology will do nothing freely for us as teachers without our directed and knowledgeable intervention with it, and a reminder that it is still all about, and always will be, great teaching and learning achieved through digital technology and not just for its own sake.

Good ILT design requires three things: know your subject, know how to teach and draw these two together through digital technology. The good news is that every teacher is two-thirds of the way there. Our glasses on this topic are already two-thirds full.

Geoff Rebbeck

Introduction

The aims of this book

This book aims to:

» explain what ILT and eLearning is in the context of the further education and skills sector;

» enable you to successfully plan, prepare, facilitate and manage ILT for learning activities and tasks related to your role;

» guide you through sourcing and applying the use of ILT and design of eLearning activities and digital resources;

» establish and encourage ways to enhance learning, teaching and assessment through the use of ILT;

» develop your digital capabilities in exploring a range of digital tools;

» identify ways to keep up to date and share your own practices of ILT.

How to use this book

Thank you and congratulations on purchasing this book. You have demonstrated your interest in knowing more about ILT and eLearning or wanting to use it more effectively. You may already be an experienced teacher or assessor, and are wanting to know about ILT or extend your use of it. As ILT can be quite a complex subject to understand, this book aims to make it more accessible to all who want to learn about it.

Have you ever thought or been told you cannot draw? Behind this barrier, the fact is we can all draw but some of us need to break down the steps in order to draw to a better level of personal satisfaction. This book will not tell you how to be an expert in ILT, as the majority of responsibility for this relies upon your teacher education, digital capabilities and creativity; however, this book will allow you to reflect on your practices and environment to understand your abilities and provide you with a foundation to build upon. Moreover, the book assumes that you are comfortable and/or willing to internet search, set up online accounts and navigate yourself around digital environments, tools, devices and services.

Many learning technology books are 'theory heavy' and are aimed at already confident ILT users and the digitally capable. You may not be where they are. If you are looking for innovative ideas or what the next big digital technology is, there are many other books available for this. This accessible text is ideal for those starting out using ILT and those who have some awareness of ILT, and are exploring how to make the most of digital technologies in their learning and teaching practices. You may even be undertaking an Education and Training programme and you need further guidance in the application of ILT. It is a useful resource to refresh on the grounding basics of how and when to use ILT effectively. The text encourages you to explore how ILT can be used in your role. This book is not theory-focused but is practical-focused, including activities and resources at the end of each chapter for you to explore further. Finally, it is firmly rooted in pedagogy and not in using technology for its own sake. The book provides practical advice through each stage of planning, designing, delivering, assessing and evaluating learning and teaching with ILT. It also includes practical advice on how you can use digital technology in your own role. While this publication is aimed at FE teachers and assessors, the text is also useful for learning technologists, trainers or support roles – anyone who is involved or interested in the enhancement of learning through the use of digital technology. In addition, much of the text can be related to Higher Education; all of the text is useful for building foundations for effective use of digital technology with any learners, as well as providing an insight into the skills and expectancies of learners coming to study with them from FE. Furthermore, learning technology businesses may also be interested to gain insights and to increase staff awareness, knowledge and skills through this book.

Taking it further

Throughout this book there are practical, reflective and exemplar activities to help you develop and think about your own practices using ILT. If you feel your skillset is beyond the text in this book, there are references, further reading and useful websites that you can explore and critically analyse where they can be applied in your practices. You may like to take the suggestions from Chapter 6 and devise/modify your own continuing professional development (CPD) plan or work with others or share your practices with others in your field of work.

The teaching and learning cycle

When planning and performing duties in your role, there are six stages that you will carry out in order for learning to be successful. This can be illustrated as an iterative cycle (see Figure 0.1), which means you will go through this more than once to achieve what you set out to do with your learners. The chapters in this book have been designed around this cycle to guide you through how ILT can be used in each stage and to reinforce important aspects for successful application.

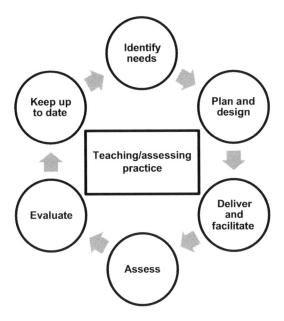

Figure 0.1. The teaching and learning cycle.
Adapted from Read and Gravells (2015)

Contact the author

If you would like to ask me anything in relation to the content of this book, please feel free to connect through Twitter with my handle @_Daniel_Scott (https://twitter.com/_Daniel_Scott) or via LinkedIn – Daniel Scott, Digital Learning Specialist (https://uk.linkedin.com/in/danielscott86).

I welcome any feedback that I will be able to use to make adjustments in future editions of this book – please contact b.danielsc@googlemail.com. Visit the blog post: http://danielscott86.blogspot.com/2018/09/learning-technology-a-handbook-for-fe-teachers-and-assessors.html to learn other ways you can leave feedback and share experiences, and join a wider community using #LTbookFE across social media. You can also learn more about the book's creation and rationale.

Reference and further reading

Read, H and Gravells, A (2015) *The Best Vocational Trainer's Guide: Essential Knowledge and Skills for Those Responsible for Workplace Learning*. Bideford: Read On Publications.

Chapter 1 Identify needs

Chapter content

This chapter covers the following topics:

» the role and purpose of Information Learning Technology (ILT), including what is ILT, eLearning and blended learning;

» ILT and eLearning in the context of the further education (FE) and skills sector;

» digital capability; including developing as a digital practitioner;

» ILT issues relating to the FE and skills sector, including barriers and FELTAG.

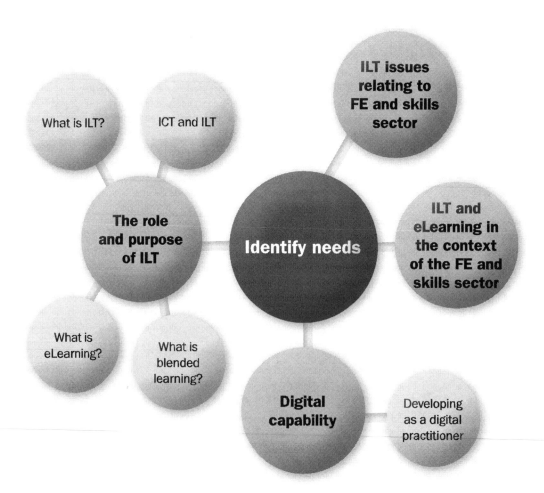

Introduction

Digital technology is an integral part of our everyday lifestyle. In this digital age, many people use digital technology without thinking of it in these terms, from accessing information at your fingertips via desktop and portable devices, to creating digital content through applications and social media. Using digital technology in education is about embracing this and converting it into learning opportunities. For example, the most meaningful learning can occur in the most informal places, such as on social media services and mobile devices, and moments of inspiration can even be found while travelling. Educators must embrace how learners of today are interacting with digital technologies and help them apply those abilities in a learning situation. Due to the digital age and easy access to a variety of free digital technologies, learners' expectations for instant and flexible online content are higher than ever. They expect and require learning materials and activities to be accessible at their fingertips. You need to use your imagination and creativity to create accessible, flexible online learning activities to reach the learners of today. This is what effective use of ILT is about, adapting learning and teaching in different ways, having instant and long-term impact for all learners, and preparing them to live and work in the current world.

ILT is simply a current expectation of teaching and learning, just like how businesses today are embracing the wealth of what digital technology brings to their organisation and teams. Education needs to welcome the positivity that ILT brings to learning experiences and teaching practices. However, including ILT in your role should not be a forced task, but something to be positively encouraged and nurtured to engage and enhance the learning, teaching and assessment journey.

Learning, teaching and assessment doesn't have to be rigid or linear. The effective use of ILT should be approached with an open mind which allows the freedom of creativity to flow. Creativity will be further developed when you have the willingness to take risks and expose what went right and wrong in the use of ILT. This allows for critical reflection and evaluation of your own practices to enable further development. You can also learn from your learners as much as they do from you. If learner feedback is taken on board, this allows for a richer experience.

ILT will not replace teachers, who will remain fundamental in encouraging, supporting and enthusing learners, as well as designing the learning process and experience. However, others in similar roles who embrace digital technology and use it effectively could potentially leave behind those that opt out, so it is important to learn and use ILT in your practices.

The role and purpose of Information Learning Technology (ILT)

It is an accepted fact that FE organisations are embracing the benefits that digital technology brings to improve and enhance the learning experience, such as flexibility and personalisation of online learning materials. Digital technology in education is referred to by a number of names such as Information Learning Technology (ILT), educational technology, technology enhanced learning (TEL) and eLearning. Collectively they all relate to the same thing, although some would see them as different parts of a process of application. The Association for Learning Technology (ALT) defines ILT as:

> " *...the broad range of communication, information and related technologies that can be used to support learning, teaching and assessment.* "
>
> **(ALT, 2018)**

ALT is based in the UK and has an international presence. It is a community of individual and corporate members that proactively research, support or enable learning through the use of learning technology. Chapter 6 provides more information about how to become a member.

New digital technologies are emerging every day which offer new and exciting ways of teaching and learning. As a result, learners expect instant and flexible access, choice and control of their learning content and materials, and are keen to personalise them to support their learning. To keep up with this growing demand, teachers face challenges such as ensuring they have the skills and appetite to use ILT effectively in their practices. Learners don't all have to face the same wall to learn any more. When applying ILT in a traditional classroom-based lesson, a common failing of inexperienced practitioners is that there is little or no underpinning pedagogical purpose. This reduces the effectiveness of what ILT could offer to enhance teaching/learning delivery, the learner experience and your own digital capabilities. ILT requires underpinning pedagogies, frameworks, plans and sometimes boundaries in order for it to have purposeful use. The main benefits that ILT brings are:

» connecting others across multiple locations;

» accessing, creating, collaborating and sharing digital information;

» increasing digital capability and skills for living and working in a digital age;

» 24/7 access to learning activities and resources in programmes, that develop with the needs of learners;

» greater choice and flexibility over place and pace of study;

» supporting a range of study types: blended, distance, work-based learning;

» providing instant opportunities for reflection and personal learning recognition;

» enabling rapid feedback on formative and summative pieces of work;

» increasing active learning with peers, through interactive and multimedia tools and resources;

» widening access to join and participate in online communities;

» enabling learning through discovery and networking.

ICT and ILT

Information communication technologies (ICT) are concerned with the use and function of electronic hardware and software. Hardware includes mobile phones and tablets, laptops, desktop computers, peripheral devices such as headsets, handsets, microphones, cameras and so on. Software consists of products and services that could be in the form of applications (apps) installed on a hardware device or accessed via websites. Multimedia is text, audio (spoken and music) and/or video (still and moving images) combined together.

Both ICT and ILT work together – one cannot work without the other, but sometimes ILT can be confused with ICT. An example is using video clips or Microsoft PowerPoint presentations as a means of embedding ILT into lessons. While these enrich learning delivery, it is not an effective use of ILT as learners are not actively involved in the process of their learning. They are just being entertained through a passive experience. ICT concerns the toolkit used, ILT is the design and application, and eLearning is the result. However, this could also be a matter of understanding and having confidence in your own ICT skills, network reliability or fear of ILT.

What is ILT?

ILT is the overall term used in FE to relate to anything 'Information Learning Technology'. It is about the overall tools and systems that can manage learning, such as publishing software, social media and virtual learning environments (VLE), a learning platform that attempts to mimic in digital alternatives everything teachers and students traditionally experience in a learning programme. ILT can be viewed as a toolkit which can help you to design learning with digital technology in mind. It should support and enhance face-to-face, blended and self-directed learning methods. In essence, it doesn't matter what technology you use, as long as the material is accessible, flexible and helps to achieve the required learning outcomes.

What is eLearning?

eLearning means electronic learning or enhanced learning. eLearning with a lower-case 'e' and uppercase 'L' signifies that 'electronic' is not the predominant process but the emphasis is on learning and pedagogy. eLearning can be viewed as peda-gogy that can be used through ILT, like a VLE for example. eLearning is a process that enables learning to be facilitated and supported appropriately within the VLE. It provides the essential pedagogical foundations that may be missing within the digital technology. eLearning can appear in many forms such as online participation activities and self-directed learning objects, often presented as an online instruction/lesson. These can be produced by the tutor or an external company. Learning objects are covered in Chapter 2. eLearning can be participated in both online and offline; the latter may offer fewer opportunities for reporting. So to summarise, ILT is the tools and systems that support and carry the pedagogy (eLearning). If designed and used well, eLearning is independent learning in disguise that promotes self-management of learning and the ability to collaborate with other learners outside of the class-room. When learners are participating in any form of eLearning, there is a significant amount of independent learning, from using and engaging with the digital technology to applying existing and new learning through it.

What is blended learning?

Blended learning is a method of delivering teaching and learning that involves a mash-up of techniques involving face-to-face learning and ILT. This means that you will still be delivering teaching and facilitating learning face-to-face, but using ILT alongside to increase learners' attention and enhance their learning uptake. There's no set formula for this; it is up to you, with the help of your learners, to decide on the right 'blend' for your programme and context.

Example

Geoff is teaching reflective theories to his learners. After he taught this he tasked his learners to use laptops or their personal electronic devices to access a shared online document, a Google Doc – that he had prepared earlier. Geoff had pre-written some questions on the Google Doc and asked his learners to work in small groups to answer them. Learners can see each other's responses and refer to this Google Doc throughout the lesson.

Another form of blended learning is the 'flipped learning/classroom'. This is an approach where the theory or introductory activity is delivered online and accessed for homework in the learners' own time. Valuable classroom time is then used to develop the knowledge further through the use of collaborative activities, allowing learners to put their knowledge into practice.

ILT and eLearning in the context of the FE and skills sector

In FE you may be given creative freedom to use ILT in any aspects of your curriculum, programme and lessons. Awarding Organisations tend to support and encourage this where possible. However, time to plan and try ILT can be very limited due to teaching, administrative and organisational pressures. Perhaps researching and practising as the programme progresses may help. While time can be restricted, to get the best out of ILT try to incorporate it into your practice as often as you can, as this will develop your knowledge as well as increase your confidence in using it. Alongside this, it's helpful to have a good understanding of your own digital capabilities, assessing what you need to learn or improve on in the use of ICT tools and systems. As a result, this will enable you to develop ideas and identify challenges which are needed to innovate – these combined can make for outstanding use of ILT.

As well as aiming for you to make effective use of ILT, the Office for Standards in Education (Ofsted) is also monitoring its impact on learning and assessment. It aims to raise standards in education and skills in the United Kingdom, for all ages, through inspections and regulatory visits, publishing the outcomes online. It is good practice to follow Ofsted guidelines even if you are not likely to be involved in an inspection. The 2017 Ofsted inspection handbook outlines that inspectors will gather evidence from the following:

» learning activities in lessons or workshops that demonstrate the use of ILT to deliver and assess learning;

» staff have appropriate expertise to design learning resources that are to the required standard and specification to support their learners;

» assistive technology to support learners to overcome barriers to learning caused by impairment or particular educational needs;

» whether learners are developing the knowledge and skills to stay safe online: know potential risks, dangers and misuse – often referred to as eSafety.

Digital capability

Digital technology can be challenging for individuals in terms of their technological and cognitive competence. These challenges include:

» practical and functional skills;

» critical thinking and evaluation;

» staying safe online;

» cultural and social understandings;

» collaborating with information;

» curating information;

» being an effective communicator;

» being creative.

Understanding your personal skill set and challenges is crucial in order to use ILT and create eLearning activities effectively. You must have good levels of digital literacies, often referred to as digital capabilities. Jisc define digital capabilities as:

> " *the capabilities which fit someone for living, learning and working in a digital society* "
>
> **(Jisc, 2017)**

Jisc is a UK-based higher and further education and skills sector not-for-profit organisation for digital services and solutions. Like ALT, they provide expert resources and events you can get involved in.

The idea of digital capabilities was developed by Jisc, and are made up of six elements: ICT proficiency (functional skills); information, data and media literacies (critical use); digital creation, problem solving and innovation (creative production); digital communication, collaboration and participation (participating); digital learning and development (development); and digital identity and wellbeing (self-actualising). You and your learners will to some degree engage with all of these elements through learning and work.

Many people are 'technology savvy' but not necessarily digitally literate. Digital literacy is about contextualising, rationalising and practising critical thinking to develop creativity and innovation with digital information, media, devices and tools. You need good digital literacy skills but it is okay to not know everything. Knowing what you don't know is important as it allows you to progress and develop. It's not always about the destination, but the journey you take while developing your skills.

Developing as a digital practitioner

As well as digital capabilities in knowing, using, creating and sharing with digital technology, there are a number of attributes that need to be developed and embraced to become an effective digital practitioner. A digital practitioner is someone who is ultimately willing and ready to embrace what ILT can bring to their role and learners' experiences. The following are attributes you can reflect on when planning and applying the use of ILT.

» **Drive** to think and work flexibly: using ILT in other ways than originally prescribed.

» **Ability** to adapt ILT to purposeful pedagogy: not viewing ILT as an 'end', but something that proactively contributes to learning and teaching.

» **Vision** to create imaginative blended learning design: learning and demonstrating creativity by re-designing learning and teaching methods to incorporate ILT.

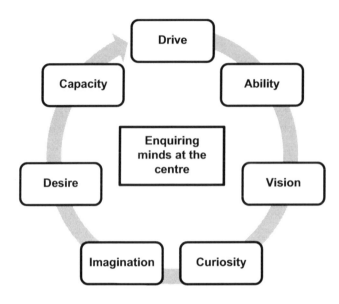

Figure 1.1. Attributes to being a digital practitioner.
Adapted from Rebbeck (2013)

» **Curiosity** to involve learners in curriculum delivery and design: including in the design and personalisation of learning.

» **Imagination** to develop future learning plans: using ILT to support learners to plan and manage their own journey.

» **Desire** to account for personal and purposeful effectiveness: using ILT to encourage and enhance reflective practice.

» **Capacity** to develop collaborative and co-operative working: scope and locate good practice internal and external to their organisation and to collaborate and assimilate ideas.

Reflective Task

» Review the attributes of the digital practitioner described in Figure 1.1. Which attributes do you feel you possess? Are there any that you feel you need to explore further? If so, how do you think you can develop these within your role?

Practical Task

» To check if you are ready for creating and embedding ILT into your subject(s), you may like to use Jisc's Online Learning Readiness Tool (https://onlineready.jisc.ac.uk).

» Alternatively, see Appendix 1.1 to see a paper-based version for you to use to assess and reflect upon your skills.

» To explore your learners' digital capabilities to use ILT, you may find it helpful to use Jisc's digital capability mapping tool in Appendix 1.2.

» Also see the websites listed at the end of the chapter where you can participate in some free online digital literacy courses to extend your understanding.

Here are some more ways in which you can increase your digital capabilities.

» Find relatable case studies like the ones Jisc have compiled for ideas on how to get started with embedding ILT into your curriculum(s), programme(s) and lesson(s): (www.jisc.ac.uk/reports/the-evolution-of-feltag or www.jisc.ac.uk/guides/developing-organisational-approaches-to-digital-capability/case-studies).

» Identify ILT champions or role models in your organisation or outside of it to ask for advice and share any good practices.

» Attend 'show and tell' style events to see how other people have embedded ILT into their practices.

» See Chapter 2 on how learning technologists can support you with any ILT-related developments and queries.

In Chapter 6 you'll discover more ways to share your own practices, collaborate with others, and discuss things you may want to try or have already tried regardless of their success. In doing so, it will help you to reflect and evaluate on recent situations, develop ways to apply ILT and think of creative ways to remove any barriers.

ILT issues relating to the FE and skills sector

There are many issues and even barriers that affect the way you use ILT in your practices – from the organisational culture through to your own personal barriers. One of the main organisational issues is posed by the Further Education Learning Technology Action Group (FELTAG). FELTAG is an influential movement and group that was commissioned by Central Government. Their agenda is: *'to make practical recommendations aimed at ensuring the effective use of digital technology in learning, teaching and assessment in Further Education and Skills'* (Hancock & Lambert, 2014, p 6).

The FELTAG report addresses how learners can increase independent study and assessment at their own pace, as well as enhancing their own digital literacy skills.

This movement has increased pressure on FE teachers and assessors, especially those that are under-skilled in this area and who are not confident in using digital technology, to adapt their curriculum to incorporate a variety of online methods. As a result, this has increased demand for training, support and inspiration for teachers and assessors to help them acquire new techniques to fulfil the requirement of a digital agenda. To ensure teachers and assessors can meet this requirement and do not simply upload numerous digital resources without considering their pedagogical purpose, the Skills Funding Agency clarified that the digital aspect means: *'when learners learn online, interact with other learners online or use online content, systems, tools and services with little, if any, direct tutor support'* (Skills Funding Agency, 2014).

It is also worth considering the process of learning itself, which produces content, useful links, new ideas, routes for exploration and so on. It is not just what the teacher produces.

Practical Task

» Access this link: https://tinyurl.com/ybpcvoma to watch these short soundbite videos.

» Select two or three videos and listen to them.

» Make notes of the key things you find interesting.

» Reflect on your notes to form an understanding of what ILT means to you and how FELTAG affects your practices and those of your organisation.

Planning and using ILT in the light of the FELTAG movement will be discussed more in Chapter 2. A way to move forward with FELTAG is to focus on your own digital capabilities and understandings of ILT mentioned in this chapter and taking on board ideas you'll read about in the subsequent chapters. In terms of your own skills and confidence, this may pose barriers to you engaging with and using ILT. You may experience a myriad of issues and obstacles; however, the common issues that arise from planning and using ILT are:

» having the time to practise using ILT;

» having the confidence to take risks;

» Wi-Fi and access to computers and devices;

» explaining/justifying the pedagogical use of ILT;

» peer support;

» technical support;

» resistance to change/change overload;

» students being open to using ILT;

» perfection in aesthetics of eLearning design;

» one size doesn't fit all;

» fear of repetition/lack of variety in teaching methods;

» access to training/CPD;

» new ILT becoming obsolete quickly;

» degree of buy-in/support from senior management;

» funding to purchase/rent ILT.

Practical Task

» Having an awareness of organisational and personal barriers determines what you can and can't achieve. There are usually solutions to every problem. If you are experiencing any of the issues in the previous bullet list, can you think of any positive ways that these can be overcome? Here are some suggestions that may help and there are more in Chapter 6:

  • Learn in your own comfort zone; choose a time and place to explore the functions and features of the tool or system and how they can be used for learning and your own development, as this will increase a sense of ownership.

  • Talk to others about what you are experiencing – two heads are better than one. Why not join an online community and view people's questions and answers in a forum?

  • Most if not all digital tools and systems have 'help' features; identify where these are.

  • Conduct an initial assessment, before your programme starts or before an activity, of your learners' skills and whether they can, or should, bring their own digital technology (smartphone, tablet), usually referred to as BYOD (bring your own device).

  • Ask your learners to show what they can do or select a 'digital mentor' to help you learn and practise new ILT.

Time is usually the first factor to consider with regard to trying new ILT, or it may be a matter of priorities. It is important to try to find time to try new digital technologies you come across. Be confident to take risks, even if they may not go to plan. Seeing them as positive failures will lead you to being confident, convinced and having a positive attitude towards ILT. However, don't take any risks where health and safety are concerned.

Reflective Task

» Map out your current digital capabilities as a diagram to make them visible.

» Think of the digital tools, apps and services you use. Open up your mobile phone to see what your most used apps are – that's a good starting point.

» Categorise them by how you use them, such as creating (document, image, video, audio), communiciating (message, group chat, networking) and consuming (news, music, receiving and dealing with information.

» Why do you carry out these particular tasks with these digital technologies? If you can find out why you don't do certain things with that particular digital technology that helps you to determine the right tool for the task, as well as identifying learning gaps and barriers.

» What would you like to do more of with that digital technology?

» Annotate your diagram by expressing how you feel about using them.

Summary

This chapter explained the role and importance of ILT and described the differences between ICT, ILT and blended learning. It introduced you to digital capabilities and considered the skills needed to become a digital practitioner and how digital practitioners are fundamental to the effective implementation of ILT. Issues and barriers to using ILT in FE were listed and you were challenged to think about how these could be overcome.

References and further reading

Association for Learning Technology (ALT) (2017) *What is Learning Technology?* [online] Available at: www.alt.ac.uk/about-alt/what-learning-technology (accessed 11 June 2018).

Bergmann, J, Overmyer, J and Willie, B (2012) *The Flipped Class: What it is and What it is Not.* [online] Available at: www.thedailyriff.com/articles/the-flipped-class-conversation-689.php (accessed 11 June 2018).

Hancock & Lambert (2014) *FELTAG Recommendations: Paths Forward to a Digital Future for Further Education and Skills.* Further Education Learning Technology Action Group.

Haythornthwaite, C and Andrews, R (2011) *E-learning Theory and Practice.* London: Sage.

Jisc (2009) *Effective Practice in a Digital Age: A Guide to Technology-enhanced Learning and Teaching.* London: HEFCE.

Ofsted (2017) *Further Education and Skills Inspection Handbook*. London: Ofsted. [online] Available at: www.gov.uk/government/publications/further-education-and-skills-inspection-handbook (accessed 11 June 2018).

Rebbeck, G (2013) *Higher Level Thinking in Using Technology-in-action (Meta Skills)*. Geoff Rebbeck.

Scott, D (2015, 11 June) *Digital Move-Meant*. [online] Available at: http://danielscott86.blogspot.com/2015/06/digital-move-meant.html (accessed 11 June 2018).

Scott, D (2016, 31 July) *Putting Learning into Learning Technology: Developing a Pedagogical Rationale to Deliver eLearning*. [online] Available at: http://danielscott86.blogspot.com/2016/10/putting-learning-into-learning-technology-developing-a-pedagogical-rationale-to-deliver-eLearning.html (accessed 11 June 2018).

Scott, D (2018, 1 February) Learning about my digital capabilities. [online] Available at: http://danielscott86.blogspot.com/2018/02/learning-about-my-digital-capabilities.html (accessed 11 June 2018).

Scott, D (2018, 6 June) Visibility matters for digital capabilities. [online] Available at: http://danielscott86.blogspot.com/2018/06/visibility-matters-for-digital.html (accessed 11 June 2018).

Skills Funding Agency (2014) *Delivering Online Learning: SFA Response to FELTAG Report*. [online] Available at: www.gov.uk/government/publications/further-education-learning-technology-action-group-recommendations-sfa-response/delivering-online-learning-sfa-response-to-feltag-report (accessed 11 June 2018).

White, D S and Le Cornu, A (2011) *Visitors and Residents: A new typology for online engagement*. [online] Available at: http://firstmonday.org/article/view/3171/3049 (accessed 11 June 2018).

White, J (2015) *Digital Literacy Skills for FE Teachers*. London: Sage.

Useful websites

» All Aboard – www.allaboardhe.ie

» Higher Education Academy – Technology-enhanced learning – www.heacademy.ac.uk/individuals/strategic-priorities/technology-enhanced-learning

» Geoff Rebbeck – www.geoffrebbeck.com

» Jisc – Building digital capability – www.jisc.ac.uk/rd/projects/building-digital-capability

» Jisc – Quick guide – Developing students' digital literacy – http://ji.sc/develop_digital_literacy

» OpenLearn – Digital literacy: Succeeding in a digital world – www.open.edu/openlearn/education-development/digital-literacy-succeeding-digital-world/content-section-overview

» The Open University – Digital and information literacy – www.open.ac.uk/library/services/digital-and-information-literacy

» The University of Edinburgh's 23 Things for Digital Knowledge – www.23things.ed.ac.uk

» University of Exeter – iTest – http://wip.exeter.ac.uk/collaborate/itest

» Digital – Learning – Culture – Visitors & Residents – http://daveowhite.com/vandr

Chapter 2 Plan and design

Chapter content

This chapter covers the following topics:

» curriculum planning for blended learning, including curriculum design for the effective use of ILT and learning design;

» sourcing ILT, including available kinds of ILT and virtual learning environments (VLEs);

» creating eLearning activities and digital resources, including instructional design, storyboarding, game-based learning and digital storytelling, authoring software, imagery, recording and audio, sourcing learning objects and open educational resources;

» making the most of learning technologists.

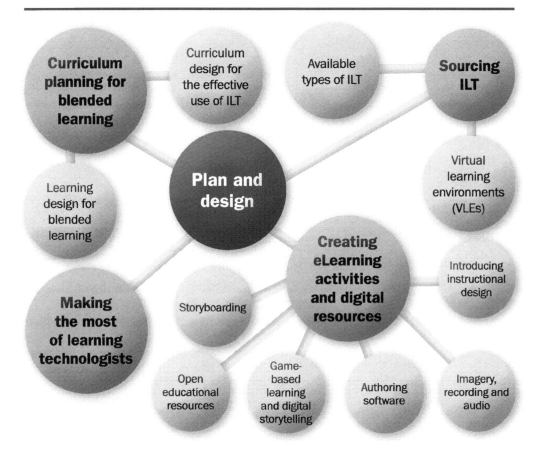

Introduction

In this chapter you will be introduced to learning design and the different kinds of ILT tools and systems that can be embedded into your curriculum, programmes and lessons. Widespread availability and instant access to online and physical digital technologies enable you to create interactive, engaging and flexible learning materials – which make your teaching methods more inclusive for learners. Learners not only participate in these but become involved in the design process. This allows you to teach in a variety of ways and formats in and out of the classroom. However, you may not always have the funds or availability of ILT resources at your disposal, so you may often be encouraged to find or even create your own digital resources and activities, resulting in additional challenges and pressures.

An important impacting factor of ILT on your role is that, if used correctly, it can reduce work time and not create more tasks. For example, one of the main benefits of 'blending' your approach is that you can copy, paste and transfer content across different applications and devices easily, and it is usually visible instantly. Also, you have more space to spread out your learning and teaching activities, and can reach a larger numbers of learners. Feedback and assessment become more instant and marking time is reduced. The positive impact on learners is that their demands are met by providing instant access to learning materials and feedback anywhere, allowing use of their own personal digital technologies, and giving them the opportunity to learn at a pace that suits their learning needs and circumstances.

The success of ILT in curriculum, programmes and lessons depends on your own attitude towards learning and using ILT with your learners. However, this relies on your understanding of pedagogies, as ILT is an extension of what is already familiar to you in your own practices. If you are confident with a range of pedagogies, this will be one less obstacle to overcome in using ILT.

Curriculum planning for blended learning

Blended learning is a mix of traditional and digital technologies that are combined together, which allows you and your learners to use time more effectively to achieve deeper learning. There are five recognised benefits to blended learning: flexibility, active learning, personalisation, learner control and feedback. Because blended learning increases flexibility, it can also have a positive impact on those learners that are hard to reach.

When delivering learning through digital technology, you will often add information to them, which is the content. In many digital technologies, the information then becomes interactive, when learners handle or take control of it. Examples are an Interactive

Whiteboard (IWB) or embedded videos on a web page. Blended learning is useful for encouraging active learning where learners can do things at the same time the teacher does – making their own sense of the experience as it happens.

There are three simple ways to use blended learning:

» **Problem-based learning** encourages active learning, using real-world scenarios, social learning and applying knowledge to new situations.

» **Social constructivism** is learning as a result of social interaction and collaboration with others.

» **Constructivism** through learners constructing their own knowledge and meaning through experience.

Blended learning allows the use of a variety of digital technologies, enabling you to dip in and out of different types of learning strategies and experiences. Digital technologies can be organised into categories in the context of learning requirements, which are introduced later in this chapter. You will still use traditional teaching methods but utilising the appropriate digital technology within these will enhance and support the teaching, and capture and present its outcomes in different ways.

Example

Rachel is an assessor in horticulture. She needs to teach her learners some basic principles before they can apply them in their workplace. As her learners' workplaces are geographically spread out, Rachel recorded herself and her presentation introducing basic principles as a short video. Rachel shared this with learners to watch through her programme site on her organisation's virtual learning environment (VLE). Rachel then used lesson time for learners to participate in structured discussions and collaborative activities around what they have learned and applied in the workplace. Therefore, instruction or theory is delivered online, which allows more time to collaborate in the lesson and discuss ways to apply knowledge in the workplace. Communication is a highly important part of blended learning as it facilitates the need to check and confirm thoughts that only happen when people interact and co-operate with others.

Curriculum design for the effective use of ILT

The traditional method of curriculum design is to identify the learning to be understood and the sequence of activities that need to be undertaken in order to achieve the learning.

Curriculum design is the same process for blended or wholly online learning and should always focus on pedagogy. These days, activities can be made more engaging and interactive, ideally involving the learner to give them ownership of the process. If designing a learner-centred curriculum, learners contributing to their own learning materials and content will be essential. Where possible, involve learners in the design process as part of your programme so that they are more invested in the learning process and don't feel their education is something 'done' to them.

Curriculum design relies on a structure such as the DADDIE model (see Figure 2.1), which demonstrates the value of the iterative design, where you will go through all stages frequently. The DADDIE model is an instructional design process that allows you to review how each piece of learning (topic) will be taught, in what sequence, what methods and tools are going to be used and the outcome.

» **Determine** is the link to curriculum design and identifies what is going to be taught and delivered.

» **Analyse** looks at the audience (learners' needs, expectations and requirements) and how they will or are likely to react to the learning process.

» **Design** takes the information obtained and allows you to create and deliver the learning in a form that is engaging and interactive. This includes the programme sequence, learning requirements, activities and assessment.

» **Develop** enables you to make your learning design a reality, and includes the resources, learning activities, and tests.

» **Implement** is about putting your learning design into action, ensuring it is accessible, inclusive and usable.

» **Evaluate** allows you to assess whether the learning design was effective or not in meeting the learning requirements.

Overall, DADDIE questions what and who it is all for, did it work and what can be done to make it better in the future. It also helps you make the best of the digital technology.

Using this brief outcome-focused process, look at what learners are expected to learn and change as a result – what they couldn't do at the beginning through to what they can do at the end.

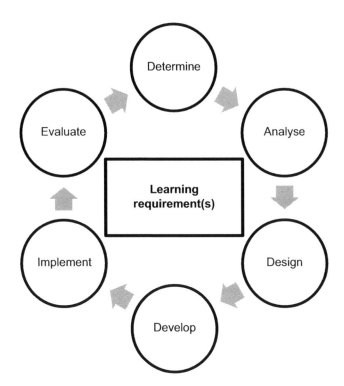

Figure 2.1. The DADDIE model, illustrating the process of executing what needs to be learned and how it will be executed.
Adapted from the ADDIE model (Branch, 2010)

Learning design for blended learning

Alongside curriculum design is a process called learning design. This is often referred to as an agile process, meaning that it is iterative; you will go through the process more than once. It is also characterised as 'design in the moment' as others (such as learners) included in the process can help set the direction of learning. Learning design should not be confused with instructional design (which involves finding efficient and creative ways of facilitating the acquisition of knowledge). Learning design is a collaborative and creative process to inform the design and decision making of the learning experience. This could be used to design a blended learning curriculum, programme and/or individual learning activities. It is useful to think of this as progressive learning, because to a degree, how a programme develops and its pace and direction are often set by what has immediately gone before in learning activity.

Curriculum design is concerned with the high-level process of defining what needs to be learned, how it will be taught, the resources available to support the learning and teaching, and how the learning will be assessed. Figure 2.2 illustrates what learning design looks like when all aspects are pulled together.

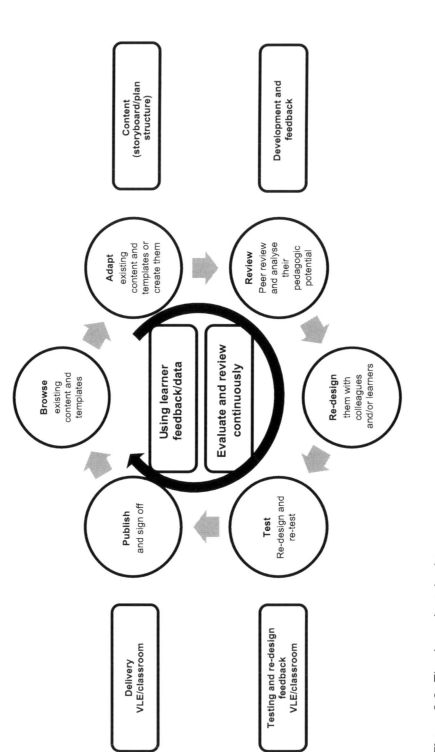

Figure 2.2. The learning design process. Adapted from Laurillard (2012)

Practical Task

» Identify and invite people that have knowledge and experience of your subject area such as other teachers, assessors and tutorial staff within your team or department and even from other sites.

» It is worthwhile inviting a learning technologist (introduced later in this chapter) and library staff. These will help you make the best out of the digital technology and pull together resources.

» Find a collaborative workspace that offers minimal interruption and gather whiteboards, pens, desktop/laptop computers and so on.

» Try to get a 'sand pit' area (a safe online space to test new features out when designing your learning activity later) created on your VLE or other online space so that you can create and test things out later.

» Use the Determine and Analyse parts of the DADDIE model previously mentioned as a way to define your learning requirements, or access this learning design word wheel to help you (www.open.edu/openlearn/wordwheel) or perhaps choose items from your scheme of work. In doing this it should help you identify what you want your learners to experience during, and what to expect after, completing your programme or lesson. These could be good principles around which to form a strategy.

» Using paper-based sticky notes or an online bulletin board like Padlet (https://padlet.com), get creative and make a storyboard of what you need to teach and divide your ideas into topics. Perhaps colour-code these to categorise them or put them into a timeline?

» Add another sticky note and describe how the topics already taught will be assessed.

» Add another sticky note and describe the ways that formative or summative assessment will be given on the assessment.

» Add a further sticky note describing a potential learning activity idea.

» Use a design template as illustrated on this website (www.gillysalmon.com/e-tivities.html) to structure your learning activity. See the example Etivity in 'Designing online activities' in Chapter 3.

» Select a digital technology that is appropriate to support the learning activity. This could be your VLE, or any of the tools suggested in the next section.

» Get others to participate in the online activity you created and ask them to give you feedback.

» Take onboard the feedback and make necessary adjustments.

For more information on this process, see 'Carpe Diem' (www.gillysalmon.com/carpe-diem.html). However, if you don't have the time to follow all of these steps, use Figure 2.3 as a quick guideline.

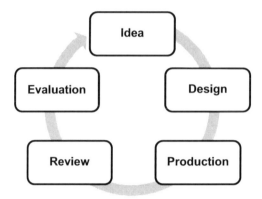

Figure 2.3. Illustrating a brief learning design process.

» Approach the learning design process as you would when creating a learning resource.

» Identify and work with experts in the subject area of the activity/programme.

» Determine your learning requirements.

» Create a storyboard or map of the content you want to include.

» Identify and use digital resources and materials.

» Select your delivery platform.

» Plan and make a prototype of your design.

» Test and review your design.

» Involve your learners or select a few to help you evaluate and gain learner feedback to improve further.

Reflection

Use the following questions to help you frame your ILT planning thinking.

» What are your learning requirements?

» Where will your learning activity take place?

» What resources do you have available?

» What digital technologies do you have available?

» What learning approaches will you take?

» What assessment and feedback strategies will you use?

» What is your learning activity and how does it achieve the learning requirements?

» Are there any follow-up activities?

» How will your learners be supported during and after your activity?

» What additional support might some of your learners need?

» How will your learners reflect on what they have learned from your activity?

» How will you reflect on the effectiveness of your activity?

Do remember that you will cycle around the learning design process multiple times. Therefore, be prepared to adapt and add to your designs as you go. The best ideas may come only after a few attempts at going through the process.

Sourcing ILT

Finding useful and cost-effective ILT can be quite a tricky task, but if you know where to search and how to assess the suitability of new ILT tools and systems this can be a straightforward thing to do. A good place to start is speaking to colleagues internally or to contacts external to your organisation who are in similar roles. See Chapter 6 for more information about this.

What makes ILT fit for purpose is the benefits it brings to learners' learning and your teaching delivery. But there are also other factors such as its ability to work successfully (usability and technically), ability to be maintained (success across different levels of programmes and learners' own abilities), capacity to function against size and volume (to be used with small and large groups of people), ability to work with existing ICT systems and networks (how ILT can work with organisational Wi-Fi and learners' own devices), and value for money.

The main benefits of ILT are as follows.

» **Time and place** – enables learning to have greater flexibility. Online resources and activities allow learners to learn at home, at work or when travelling, as well as in their designated place of learning at times that best suit them.

» **Pace of learning** – learners have more control over the pace and place of their own learning and can better integrate it into their lives, personalising their own learning preferences.

» **Variety and flexibility of learning** – learners can interact with others around the world and do individual or group work, or blend their own digital, physical and social learning.

» **Content focus** – digital activities and resources are easily adaptable for learners with specific needs or preferences.

» **Differentiation** – learners' diverse needs can be met through assistive technologies and open educational resources (OERs) – explained later in this chapter.

» **Your use of time** – you can distribute time in different ways to deliver whole-class, small group, and individual support, across face-to-face and online learning. A consequence of this is that you may find your lesson plans stretch over longer periods of time rather than over a given lesson.

» **Digital skills** – learners will develop these through use of ILT; useful for future employment and in searching, refining and understanding online information.

Choosing the right digital technology is like finding the right tool for the job. For example, a bricklayer would need a trowel to help build a wall. They wouldn't choose a spade to help them achieve this. As there is a wealth of digital technologies out there that are suitable for a wide range of ILT requirements, there will be a suitable tool for any occasion. Here are some quick questions to ask yourself when assessing new ILT you come across.

Reflection

» What is the main purpose of this digital technology?

» How can I use it and what features can I use to deliver my teaching through it?

» What and how will learners access and interact with it?

» How does pedagogy blend into the digital technology?

» Carry out an initial assessment of what learners are bringing into the classroom and beyond. How can learners use their own personal devices to enhance their own learning experience?

» Identify and analyse potential risks, issues and problems of the digital technology. Always have a back-up plan just in case it doesn't work.

Refer back to Chapter 1 to revisit how you can build confidence in using digital technology. Remember, it is good to focus on what you can do with digital technology rather than what you can't. However, be aware of its limitations.

Available types of ILT

In terms of delivering your learning or teaching content, you need to decide what appropriate digital technologies you can use in line with your learning objectives or what your learners need to achieve. The following will help you identify how to best approach the digital technology you would like to use.

» **Acquisition/assimilative** – reading text, watching a video, listening to audio.

» **Discussion/communicative** – articulating ideas, questions and challenging and responding to others.

» **Investigative** – finding, handling and dealing with information.

» **Practice/experiential** – applying learning into a work or formal setting (learning by doing or learning through experience).

» **Collaborative/interactive** – participating, sending, receiving and exchanging information to help produce something.

» **Productive** – producing something tangible and contextual that demonstrates current knowledge and skills.

You will come across many different kinds of digital technologies that have different purposes. It's about choosing the right tool for the job. With this in mind, there are two general categories of digital technologies that operate in different ways to each other. Figure 2.4 illustrates the following descriptions of the two genres you will come across to help you decide which ones best suit your needs.

» **Asynchronous** – happening at different times at the same place. For example, a tutor has set up a topic for discussion during the course of the week in an online forum on a VLE. Learners participate in the forum discussion at a time to suit them. Learners may be in different geographical locations and time zones but are still able to access and participate.

» **Synchronous** – happening in real time for all at the same place. For example, a tutor using Microsoft Skype (www.skype.com) to video call a learner for a one to one. Both tutor and learner could be in different geographical locations but are participating at the same time.

ASYNCHRONOUS   SYNCHRONOUS

Figure 2.4. Illustrating asynchronous and synchronous digital technologies.

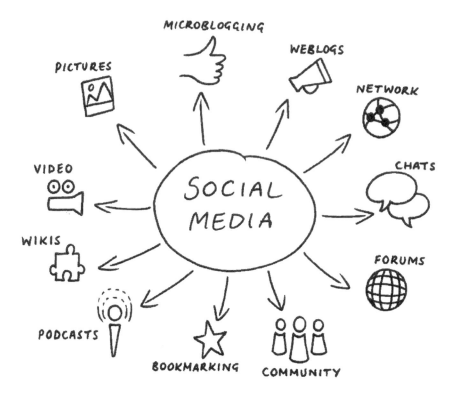

MICROBLOGGING

WEBLOGS

PICTURES

NETWORK

VIDEO

CHATS

WIKIS

FORUMS

PODCASTS

BOOKMARKING   COMMUNITY

Figure 2.5. Illustrating the types of social media that you will come across.

Social media offers great tools and services to connect with others and gather information rapidly. They can be used asynchronously and synchronously.

Social media (as Figure 2.5 illustrates) enables the sharing of 'in the moment' activities, issues and learning. It can yield a 'long conversation' that lasts for the life of the course and provides sociability for a class. Social media provides a simple platform for others to be inspired and generate ideas anytime and anywhere. It can also support the administration of learning. The 'social' aspect means interacting, giving and receiving information through verbal and non-verbal means for the purpose of acquiring something. The 'media' aspects relate to websites and applications that enable users to create and share content or to participate in social networking. However, there is also a wide range of digital tools that are categorised under the following themes.

» **Multimedia production** – making videos or animations at a basic level. YouTube Creator Studio (www.youtube.com) is attached to your YouTube account. It is a simple way to create effective instructional videos.

» **Delivery** – digital technology in the classroom: VLE, lecture capture, Office 365 (www.office.com), Google Drive (www.google.com/drive), visualiser (a modern projector).

» **Presentation** – presenting your learning and teaching content in a visual way: Prezi (https://prezi.com) and Haiku Deck (www.haikudeck.com) can make visually appealing presentations.

» **Collaboration** – allowing people to work together on a shared outcome (at the same time or not): Office 365/Google Drive have online documents that you can create and share with learners.

» **Reflective** – allowing you to record your thoughts and feelings and recall them when needed. Google Blogger (www.blogger.com) is an excellent tool to create a blog site and personalise it the way you want. Similar tools: Twitter (https://twitter.com) and Tumblr (www.tumblr.com).

» **Interactive** – eLearning objects that contain activities and animations that enable learners to participate beyond simple reading and thinking tasks. H5P (https://h5p.org) is a useful tool to achieve this.

» **Social** – enabling discussions through your VLE forum, Yammer (via Office 365) (www.yammer.com) or other social media to share knowledge and skills with peers and the wider world. Learning doesn't exclusively occur in classrooms, but digitally in various online networks and environments. The social aspects of learning are very important in helping hold a class together where learners are typically in work placements or learning at distance.

» **Curation** – finding and collating digital resources and categorising them the way you like through tools like Pearltrees (www.pearltrees.com), Pinterest (www.pinterest.com), Scoop.it (www.scoop.it) and Evernote (https://evernote.com).

You are likely to have access to a range of ILT that you may not be aware of or have considered using. In most educational organisations there is typically access to a virtual learning environment (VLE) of some kind, which is discussed later in this chapter. You may also have items such as IWBs, touch screen display devices, a visualiser, a lecture capture system and access to cloud-based platforms/storage and online collaborative documents like Microsoft Office 365/Google Drive applications. These digital technologies are a great way to get started in making digital activities and resources, so try to make the most of what you have available. You may want to contact your information technology department and ask them how you can access these digital technologies. Remember that learners also have their own digital technologies and preferences. They may want to bring and use their own devices to help with their learning.

Practical Task

» Access the C4LPT website (http://c4lpt.co.uk) and navigate to the Tools Directory section.

» Select the category of digital technologies you would like to explore.

» You can also access the Top 200 Tools, which lists the most popular digital technologies.

» Select a digital technology and review the description to see what its main function is.

» If you like the sound of it, then select the title to take you to its main website to explore further and reveal its possibilities.

» Try creating an account and exploring all of the features it offers.

» Create a mock example activity or a mock resource to get a feel of its potential.

» Perhaps make a wish list or a resource bank to refer back to.

» Chat to a colleague about what ILT they use in their practices and to your information technology department to discover what is available for you to use.

Practical Task

» Think about 'who, what, why, when, where, how' as a rationale to planning the use of ILT. However, it is important not to let digital technology rule over pedagogy. See Appendix 2.1, Quick ILT Planner, to help you put together a plan of action.

Virtual learning environments

Virtual learning environments (VLEs) are a popular digital technology within many educational organisations that enable learners to log in and access online activities and resources that you have uploaded. VLEs attempt to replicate traditional classroom activity as well as supporting aspects of it when the physical classroom isn't available. VLEs are ideal platforms for hosting blended, flipped, self-directed and distance-learning activities. You may already know which VLE your organisation uses, but if not, it would be useful to find out. Most if not all VLEs operate with similar functions and features. The VLE is an excellent starting point for blended learning; however, you need to have adequate digital literacy skills to use the eLearning tools to create digital activities and resources for your learners. VLEs enable you to make learning and teaching content available beyond the classroom walls. If you don't want to create accounts on various external websites, VLEs come with effective eLearning tools within them, which makes them a very popular choice among educators. It's a case of understanding the kinds of eLearning tools and how to use them within the system. Table 2.1 illustrates what most VLEs may look like and include.

Table 2.1. Illustrating a typical VLE programme layout and features within it.

User profile/profile settings					
Programme title/lesson title and organisation					
Programme summary/schedule/learning requirements					Assignment deadlines
Your contact details VLE guidelines/ground rules					Programme updates/ announcements
Programme discussion forum					Quick access resources
Topic 1/week 1					Programme/ organisation social media link(s)
Introduction	• Video tutorials • Interactive activities • Links to other learning activities • Suggested reading	• Topic discussion forum • Production of content	Quizzes	Summary/ review of topic	Reading list
					Glossary
					Technical help

The following are some popular free and fee-based VLE services that you can explore:

» Blackboard Learn – www.blackboardlearn.com

» Canvas – www.canvasvle.co.uk

» CourseSites – www.coursesites.com

» Edmodo – www.edmodo.com

» Educadium – www.educadium.com

» Moodle – https://moodle.org

» Simple VLE – www.simplevle.com

Table 2.2 opposite outlines the kinds of activities you may expect to find in a VLE with examples of how to use the features. It incorporates the types of learning approaches using ILT, as introduced earlier, and references Bloom's taxonomy. Bloom's taxomomy is an ordered and hierarchical collection of terms that characterise the ways learning can be demonstrated by learners. They are verbs that are used to encourage higher-order thinking and learning, in both learning and teaching activities.

Here are some common tools you may find in your VLE.

» **File** – an individual text, image, video file.

» **Folder** – files can be put into a folder to reduce information overload and scrolling.

» **Glossary** – you and the learners can enter course-related words to refer to or hyperlink to those words that appear on the whole site.

» **Label** – a space to add text or image to break up your content.

» **Page** – a blank web page for you to enter multimedia or learning content.

» **Quiz** – create multiple choice, text entry, drag and drop, matching questions for formative or summative assessment or exams.

» **Online lesson** – upload eLearning objects and have any scores recorded.

» **Questionnaire/Survey** – design initial assessments, capture feedback, reflections.

» **Websites** – insert links to websites that are useful to the study subject or signposting for additional information.

Table 2.2. Typical features and functions available in a VLE.

Pedagogy – different types of learning in action through;	Acquisition/assimilative	Discussion/communicative	Investigative	Practice/experiential	Collaborative/interactive	Productive
Bloom's taxonomy	**Understanding – explain ideas or concepts** (Explain, describe, determine, interpret, summarise, differentiate)	**Analysing – draw connections among ideas** (Compare, contrast, categorise, calculate, criticise, question)	**Remembering – recall facts and basic concepts** (Define, identify, review, report, label, list, name, state, match, recognise, select, recall)	**Applying – use information in new situations** (Apply, solve, modify, use, demonstrate, experiment, relate, prepare, practice, carry out, administer)	**Evaluating – justify a stand or decision** (Evaluate, reflect, assess, judge, appraise, decide, measure, consider, critique, justify)	**Creating – produce new or original work** (Plan, design, create, produce, construct, develop, devise, adapt, assemble, manage)
Book	• Reading text in short and long paragraphs • Embed video players into sequenced chapters • Embed video links as hypertext • Embed audio links as hypertext	• Embed/place book link into discussion forum for review and discussion resource	• Breaking up lots of information into chapters • Condensing information into one area	• Introduce information in a chapter and place instructional questions testing understanding afterwards (info > activity > info activity)	• Group activity in a collaborative document to write up content for their own book resource using programme materials and research	• Enable editing rights for learners to co-create their own book/article

Pedagogy – different types of learning in action through;	Acquisition/ assimilative	Discussion/ communicative	Investigative	Practice/ experiential	Collaborative/ interactive	Productive
Chat/ discussion forum	· Reading through chat logs and providing a summary or reflection of own understanding · Download the chat log and analyse and interpret for assignments	· Discussing and sharing knowledge gained in topics · Confirming projects, tasks, content	· Sourcing and sharing useful and relevant resources with peers	· Discussing ways to use new knowledge and techniques in own practices	· Informative tutorial discussions · Scheduled question and answer · Drop-in question and answer · Live group debates · Guest speaker	· Create a narrative or supporting narrative to project work
Choice	· Check understanding like a multiple choice question · Critical questioning on choices they would make in relation to a scenario	· Make all learner choices visible to everyone for them to discuss	· Participants to choose a range of options, module choices, tutorial bookings and so on	· Choices learners would make in relation to a given scenario or case study	· Peer assess other learner's choices to a given set of criteria	· Enable editing rights for learners to co-create their own choice activity

Pedagogy – different types of learning in action through;	Acquisition/ assimilative	Discussion/ communicative	Investigative	Practice/ experiential	Collaborative/ interactive	Productive
Database	• Retrieve and review entered information	• Discuss entries and findings with others	• Learners to carry our research and log findings into a database	• Categorise findings to make sense of the information • Use findings to apply into a project or task	• Share and disseminate findings with others	• Learners manage their own database and information
Wiki	• Brainstorm, enter, review, refine and structure content onto the web pages	• Learning reflecting on what they created and how it can be improved	• Agree on content and transferring content from other sources	• Content of the web pages are usable for others in their context	• Learners discussing and collaborating on making changes to content	• Learners to ensure this body of work is fit for outside audiences • The web pages can be a resource for future cohorts

Practical Task

Use the following checklist to help you include essential aspects of your online programme that sits within your VLE or other platform. Some you may be able to do yourself, for others you may need to contact your VLE administrator.

Programme site structure

☐ Set format of the programme (topics, weekly).

☐ Add any essential features or remove any that are unnecessary.

☐ Site structure represents your programme structure.

Programme information

☐ Online programme is named appropriately according to the programme structure.

☐ Programme description is available.

☐ Programme learning objectives are visible and clear.

☐ Programme assessment details and submission and feedback processes are visible and clear.

☐ Programme policies/procedures your learners are expected to comply with are clearly stated.

☐ Minimum access requirements are clearly stated and instructions for use provided for learners.

☐ Instructions are clear on how to get started and where to find various information and activities.

☐ Programme guidelines (expectations) for online discussions and email are clearly stated.

☐ Video introduction from you and subsequent topics if possible.

☐ Contact information of when and how to be contacted.

☐ Expected response time for contact details shown.

☐ Tutor roles are visible and described within the programme site.

Access

☐ Programme is open and accessible to learners.

☐ You have access to programmes you are delivering and assessing on.

☐ You have correct permissions to facilitate and manage learners' learning.

☐ Learners are enrolled on the programme site.

☐ Learners are assigned correct role to particpate as required.

Interaction and activities

☐ Activities and resources are named appropriately, for example with week number and topic.

☐ Files have meaningful names, for example, 'Programme name' – Lesson 1 – Lesson 1 Introduction.pptx.

☐ Created an introduction/welcome announcement in the programme forum/news section.

☐ Introductory activity or content is available to complete.

☐ Enabled: announcements, appropriate spaces for programme content, reading lists.

☐ Documents are viewable and open up correctly.

☐ Recorded lessons/webinars are embedded and open correctly.

☐ All hyperlinks are correct and open up correctly.

☐ Check any conditional settings are linked to activities to ensure they meet criteria for a digital badge.

☐ Check access and restriction dates are correct.

☐ Quiz weightings/scores are set appropriately.

☐ Content conforms to copyright legislation (www.legislation.gov.uk/ukpga/1988/48/contents).

Accessibility and usability

☐ Fonts and styles are consistent.

☐ Colour schemes and icons in activities are consistent and meet accessibility requirements.

☐ Labels are used to aid navigation throughout the programme.

☐ Alternative formats are provided that meet the needs of diverse learners.

☐ Large files are identified to help learners consider their data/download allowance, as well as web page timeout issues.

☐ Large graphics are optimised for viewing more easily.

Creating eLearning activities and digital resources

Creating eLearning activities and digital resources can be one of the most time-consuming aspects of making your learning material online. But it's very worthwhile as it makes your curriculum, programmes and lessons more dynamic, and once created they may only need modifying in subsequent years. eLearning has to be designed and delivered differently to face-to-face. What works well in a classroom may not necessarily work well when accessed online. Digital activities are best used with blended and flipped learning approaches that complement both digital and face-to-face methods. If you feel confident, then you could create your own digital activities and resources. You may be looking to provide some self-paced learning activities on your VLE space or on another digital platform. Or you may be even thinking about converting your presentations/lectures into videos or taking your paper-based materials and making instructional videos.

eLearning objects are a good way to consolidate your learning and teaching content into one self-paced online activity. Typically, learners will be presented with aims and objectives and guided through information, enabling you and them to check their learning during and towards the end. eLearning objects promote the benefits of flexibility, personalisation and independence – being learner-centred. If you have time, try to be original and authentic when creating your own eLearning content and innovate by developing something new to you and your learners. The following will provide you with a framework to work to and tools and resources to help you through the design and development.

Introducing instructional design

Earlier in this chapter the DADDIE model was introduced as a way to scope your learning content and design for blended delivery. This model is popular in instructional design because it takes you through the whole eLearning design cycle from conception to implementation. This prompts you to think of your audience and who you are designing for.

Two vital components to learning online are how you present information and how you will facilitate learning throughout. Instructional design is a process that typically starts with an analysis of defining a learning need. The process continues by deciding how to structure and present the required learning for the audience defined in the analysis. Prototyping and testing follows to ensure success and usually ends with an evaluation for quality assurance and future developments. Instructional design is often underpinned by Gagné's nine events of instruction to create engaging and meaningful instruction. Further details can be found in the 'References and further reading' section at the end of the chapter or search online to get an insight into the nine areas.

You may also need to think about:

» identify subject matter experts (SMEs)/key person(s) to review/check the quality of the products on an ongoing basis;

» agree quality-checking process of each eLearning object;

» agree content outline; titles, flow of content – perhaps in Microsoft PowerPoint;

» only keep the text that is essential as long text will be chunked, resulting in more slides;

» supply questions, answers and feedback to any quizzes or short-answer questions;

» sources of any additional high-quality logos, images and/or video clips that are related or useful to the content.

Storyboarding

Storyboarding is a visual method that helps you specify the flow of content and interaction by creating a process of what happens from beginning to end, which you build later. There are many ways to create a storyboard, following the advice about learning design earlier in the chapter: wireframes (three-dimensional line drawings illustrating a process or structure) or simply using Microsoft PowerPoint to illustrate content pages. Microsoft PowerPoint is a good start for making a storyboard of what you want in each section and outlining how you want learners to interact with it. You could also print off blank slides with the note section. To get some further guidance on storyboarding for eLearning, visit The eLearning Coach article: http://theelearningcoach.com/elearning_design/storyboards-for-elearning. However, you may want to find out which creative ways to design eLearning may be easier for you. Perhaps you'd like to sketch the 'look and feel' out, and then make it into reality.

To help you, consider the following questions.

» What pedagogical problems are you trying to solve?

» What do learners need to do/complete/evidence?

» What do you and learners need to get out for the assessment?

» Think critically of 'who, what, why, when, where, how'.

» Also think about:

  • The end result in mind.

  • What learning instruction, feedback methods and assessment it will have.

  • What are you asking learners to do or think about?

  • What software/tool features would you use?

  • What instructions, guidance or resources would you include?

  • Whether any learning check points are required.

» Outline titles, the flow of content to appear in each section, and trim out unnecessary material.

» Divide learning content into relatable groups of knowledge.

» Annotate and describe any activities you wish to include so that learning can be assessed and checked.

» Decide the layout and formats to present the learning digitally.

You can be creative using software; however, sometimes it may restrict your flexibility. Sketch a storyboard of what you want the online activity to look like. Annotate the storyboard with the most appropriate pedagogy, learning activities and assessment methods. It's an authentic way to creatively design something and then apply the necessary components. Put yourself in the mind of a learner or even a tutor. Imagine you are delivering this online: what would work for you and your learners? Understand the activity and how best you can deliver it online, taking in account the needs and expectations of learners. A few points to note when developing your content are as follows.

» Be mindful of putting too much content in as this can lead to information overload. Equally, including too many interactions can lead to user fatigue.

» Don't put too much text on screen as it makes it very text-based and may make the object longer. Only keep essential text and present in small bitesize chunks. Or provide an option saying 'read more'.

» Use relatable images to match your text.

» Use video and interactive elements to make content engaging and meaningful.

You can make you content interactive by considering the following options, as well as discovering more by exploring the software/tool you are using, or even by experiencing an eLearning object yourself.

» **Animation** – a simulation of movement created by displaying a series of pictures or frames. This includes embedding videos or animated graphics.

» **Quizzes and puzzles** – for example, drag and drop; fill in the blank questions; flashcards; guess the answer; hotspot; matching; memory game; mulitple choice questions; true or false questions.

» **Repeat interaction** – users can repeat what they have done, such as rewinding a video or animation, or reattempting questions.

» **Roll over/click boxes** – areas on the eLearning object over which users can hover to view information. They must click before the next action to take place.

» **Show progress** – forward or onward movement towards a destination; for example, a graphic showing the sections and activities completed.

If you are creating eLearning on the go, the following is a quick framework for structuring content that includes key instruction and assessment principles. It's about being short, sharp and straight to the point.

» Aims and objectives (what learners will learn)

» Introduction/build-on from previous learning

  • Bitesize theory/interaction

  • Formative assessment activity

  • Bitesize theory/interaction

  • Formative assessment activity

» Summative assessment

» Aims and objectives (what learners have learned)

However, when designing eLearning content to be viewed on mobile devices, some digital technologies will resize and reformat content to fit automatically. When making any digital content, be mindful of how it will be accessed by your learners. Try to design-in accessibility, flexibility and portability, regardless of the device or operating system that it might be viewed on. Personal preference should be enabled to allow choice when in the mindset for learning. To improve the user experience of your eLearning objects, have a look at the following articles.

» Usability.gov – Visit User Experience Basics – www.usability.gov/what-and-why/user-experience.html

» Usability.gov – Usability Evaluation Basics – www.usability.gov/what-and-why/usability-evaluation.html

Sign up to The eLearning Coach newsletter, to receive useful articles linking to ideas and resources for creating eLearning materials (http://theelearningcoach.com).

Game-based learning and digital storytelling

Game-based learning, often referred to as gamification, is simply adding game design, thinking and mechanics to non-game situations. Game-based learning offers other important lessons for learners around choices and consequences and is often used in teaching life skills. You may already have added some sort of gaming element to non-digital activity to encourage engagement, motivation and positive behaviour among learners. The same principles apply when converting this digitally. In eLearning there are a few ways you can gamify your materials.

» **Open badges** – in your VLE you may have options to add badges to specific activities or quizzes which will be issued once criteria have been met. If your VLE does issue badges and you have permission to create and upload your own unique badges to use, access this site (www.openbadges.me).

» **Points** – look to where you can add individual or team points to activities and resources and make the leaderboard visible to everyone.

» **Rewards** – how can learners use the points; is there a prize of some sort or unlocking another activity?

If you don't feel ready to get involved in creating your own games, do some internet searching on educational games or generators to make instant activities.

Like game-based learning, you can add storytelling elements to your learning materials to make them more exciting. Digital storytelling is often applied to eLearning objects to make them more interesting and relatable. You can do this by thinking what is the story or scenario about? Is there an issue or conflict? Who are the characters? Think about how you can link the learning to these aspects and messages. Make both story and characters relatable to create curiosity and intrigue. Enable interaction: can they choose their character and do they have different outcomes? Think of branching in terms of how learners answer a question and whether it needs to take them down another pathway. How does the ending meet the learning requirements set at the beginning and throughout? Does it have a closed or open ending, leaving the virtual-door open for a sequel? Be mindful not to overcomplicate the story and create cognitive overload. Keep key points clear and visible so they don't get lost in the story or even become the story. Perhaps you may know a colleague from a drama or theatre background to help script a brief story?

Authoring software

There is a wide choice of authoring software that you can use to create eLearning content. Many are quite similar in what they offer; there are free ones and some are quite costly. You have the option of downloading, subscribing or accessing the software via cloud-based platforms. You may need to learn skills in using this kind of authoring software; however, you can search online for communities of help and YouTube for self-help tutorials. Access the following site that lists a comprehensive range of authoring software that you might want to investigate further (http://c4lpt.co.uk/directory-of-learning-performance-tools/instructional-tools). H5P (https://h5p.org) is a particularly effective and free tool to try out; it is highly accessible on multiple devices and VLEs.

Imagery, recording and audio

Using images on your VLE site or eLearning object to break up text is a good way to increase engagement as well as making it look appealing. Finding suitable and relevant images and being able to use them in your materials can be quite tricky due to copyright restrictions. Access some of the following popular sites or this list for further ones (http://c4lpt.co.uk/directory-of-learning-performance-tools/image-galleries-photo-sharing-sites). Some may be free and again some are available on a subscription basis.

» Compfight – http://compfight.com

» Everystockphoto – www.everystockphoto.com

» Morguefile – https://morguefile.com

» Pik Wizard – https://pikwizard.com

» Stock Up – www.sitebuilderreport.com/stock-up

» Unsplash – https://unsplash.com

» Wikimedia Commons – https://commons.wikimedia.org

A quick way to find reusable images is by using filtered options on Google Images. Access Google Images, enter your search query, go to 'Tools' on the right-hand side, then to 'Usage' rights underneath and select 'Labelled for reuse'. This will bring up all images that you can reuse in your materials.

You can make your own videos to use in or out of your classroom in a number of ways. You could add a video of you narrating your teaching presentation slides to then put on your VLE. Presuming you have a webcam, you can record a video of you talking through your material. If you would like a standalone video of you introducing a topic and/or giving a tutorial on a resource you have found, you could use screencast software such as Screencast-O-Matic (https://screencast-o-matic.com) or via the 'Recording Tab' in Microsoft PowerPoint. If you have access to a lecture capture system, this will allow you to do the same. You can further edit your videos with minimum effort using free video editing software like Windows Movie Maker or use YouTube's Creator Studio.

Why not enhance your digital content further by adding narration, music or sound effects? You can find a useful list of services and software here (http://c4lpt.co.uk/directory-of-learning-performance-tools/audio-podcast-tools).

Open educational resources

Open educational resources (OERs) are digital resources: objects and artefacts which are created, uploaded, shared and re-purposed among learning, teaching and assessment communities. You can find relatable OERs by searching on the internet by your subject and the terms 'resources' or 'OERs'. Some websites may ask you to create an account or subscribe. You can upload and access OERs on your VLE or access via mobile devices. If you do use or re-purpose an OER, you are encouraged to reciprocate by sharing a resource of your own. If you decide to share a resource you have created, visit (https://creativecommons.org) to learn how to create copyright-free licences to give people permission to use and share your work. Attribution in the context of OERs means that you need to acknowledge the creator of materials when you use them. Your learners could create their own OERs as part of an activity or for curriculum and programme resources. This allows them to contribute knowledge and skills to the subject and wider community. The following are some popular sites where you can find OERs for your subject area(s). You can even use social media channels using relevant hashtags to increase searchability, discoverability and retrieval.

» Jisc – App and resource store – https://store.jisc.ac.uk/home

» Khan Academy – www.khanacademy.org

» Merlot II – www.merlot.org/merlot/index.htm

» MIT OpenCourseWare – https://ocw.mit.edu/index.htm

» NLN Learning Materials – https://xtlearn.net/NLN

» OER Commons – www.oercommons.org

» OpenLearn – www.open.edu/openlearn

» The Excellence Gateway – www.excellencegateway.org.uk

» Videojug – www.videojug.com

Making the most of learning technologists

If your time is too limited or you feel you are not ready to design and create your own digital activities and resources, fear not. You will probably have specialists in your organisation that could help you immensely in using ILT and creating digital activities and resources.

In your organisation, these specialists may be called eLearning designers/developers, educational/VLE developers, instructional designers or learning technologists. Simply put, a learning technologist is a mediator between pedagogy, design and learning delivery – helping to bring digital technology into purposeful pedagogy. They develop digital learning materials for blended and online learning and will work with you to plan, create and support you in the use of innovative learning materials and course design.

While learning technologists understand complex aspects of digital technology, they are often qualified in teaching – which can be a huge benefit to the role! They are educationalists, who aim to improve learning and teaching with technology. Each learning technologist is different in every organisation and they will be adaptable and flexible, moulding to their organisational surroundings and/or subjects they deal with. This is key as it enables you to delve into the subject and collaborate with experts so that you can explore the proposed programme content, hear their suggestions and work with them to evaluate the right digital technologies. Learning technologists are also responsible for driving change. Without them organisations run the risk of using the same old digital technology for the same purpose, which can demotivate both learner and teacher. This also doesn't help further the cause that digital technology enhances learning and teaching practices. A good learning technologist acts as a mediator between the pedagogy and technology. It's a delicate process of translation between teaching methods and digital technology.

In most situations it is the learning technologist that leads and facilitates the creativity and implementation of ILT. Learning technologists typically direct the use of ILT and creation of eLearning while the tutor guides the pedagogy or instruction. You could see it as 'help them to help you' when time is very limited to develop your own digital resources or even set up ICT tools for use in the classroom. The following lists ways that a learning technologist can help you or how you can approach them. This is not exhaustive and your list may include a lot more depending on the context of the organisation:

» Desire to support you to plan, set up and deliver through ILT.

» Knowledge and awareness of:

- impact and evaluation of ILT and eLearning;
- current global markets and trends in eLearning and practices;
- online tools and resources;
- apps;
- devices (mobiles, tablets, laptops, IWB, digital cameras, lecture capture, visualiser);
- accessibility;
- copyright;
- General Data Protection Regulation (GDPR) – covered in Chapter 5.

» Identify pedagogical need/issue.

» Identify gaps where improvements can be made.

» Ask about the activity/purpose (this is your responsibility too).

» Build a demo/mock eLearning example if necessary.

» Suggest a choice of approaches to use the application/tool and let you decide which best suits your needs.

» Guided walkthrough demo of application/tool on letting you design, create or set up.

» Respond appropriately and positively to situations and change.

» Curate relevant knowledge, skills, resources, people and places.

» Help you to improve your digital capabilities.

» Ask to be involved in departmental meetings to advise on ILT-related areas.

» Collaborate with you on suggesting ideas, being involved in your lesson and developing your programme further.

» Visualise an idea then analyse and evaluate how they can use it and apply it to your purposes.

» Follow up discussions with further advice and resources.

» Networking at internal and external events – asking others what they do and decide how you can use their expertise.

» Connect with others – initiate/mediate professional networking relationships.

» Keep up to date with what others do – sourcing latest information and good practice internally and externally to the organisation.

» Publish and promote their work and findings through blogs, social media and websites.

Summary

This chapter reiterated the importance of curriculum design and introduced a learning design methodology to assist in creating effective blended learning opportunities, the types of digital technologies and ways that you can source them. Methods to create your own digital activities and resources were introduced, along with encouraging the possibilities of working collaboratively with your learning technologists to help you use ILT more effectively.

References and further reading

Association for Project Management (2014) *Introduction to Gamification*. Princes Risborough, Buckinghamshire: Association for Project Management.

Beetham, H and Sharpe, R (2013) *Rethinking Pedagogy for a Digital Age* (3rd edition). London: Routledge.

Branch, R M (2010) *Instructional Design: The ADDIE Approach*. New York: Springer.

Gagné, R M, Briggs, L J and Wager, W W (1992) *Principles of instructional design (4th ed)*. Fort Worth, TX: Harcourt Brace Jovanovich College Publishers.

Hopkins, D (2015) *The Really Useful #EdTechBook*. Atascadero, CA: CreateSpace Independent Publishing Platform.

Horton, S (2005) *Access by Design: A Guide to Universal Usability for Web Designers*. Berkeley, CA: New Riders.

Horton, W (2011) *e-Learning by Design* (2nd edition). Hoboken, NJ: John Wiley & Sons.

Jisc (2009) *Effective Practice in a Digital Age: A Guide to Technology-enhanced Learning and Teaching*. London: HEFCE.

Jisc (2009) *Managing Curriculum Change: Transforming Curriculum Design and Delivery through Technology*. London: HEFCE.

Laurillard, D (2012) *Teaching as a Design Science: Building Pedagogical Patterns for Learning and Technology*. London: Routledge.

Mayer, R E (2003) The Promise of Multimedia Learning: Using the Same Instructional Design Methods Across Different Media. *Learning and Instruction*, 13: 125–39.

Mayer, E R and Moreno, R (2003) Nine Ways to Reduce Cognitive Load in Multimedia Learning. *Educational Psychologist*, 38(1): 43–52.

Mayes, T and de Freitas, S (2004) *Review of e-Learning Theories, Frameworks and Models*. [online] Available at: https://tinyurl.com/ycfzgahb (accessed 11 June 2018).

Oliver, M (2002) *What do Learning Technologists Do? Innovations in Education and Training International*, 39(4): 245–52.

Pratt, D, Schmoller, S, Jennings, D, Buckman, W, Bush, M, Squire, D and Wes, N (2017) *A Design Guide for Open Online Courses*. [online] Available at: http://repository.alt.ac.uk/2373/1/DesignGuideOpenOnlineCourses1-4.pdf (accessed 11 June 2018).

Quality Matters (2014) *Quality Matters Rubric Standards Fifth Edition, 2014, with Assigned Point Values* (5th edition). Maryland Online, Inc.

Quinn, C N (1996) *Pragmatic Evaluation: Lessons from Usability*. 13th Annual Conference of the Australasian Society for Computers in Learning in Tertiary Education, Australasian Society for Computers in Learning in Tertiary Education.

Rebbeck, G (2016) *String Learning: Blend and Learning Objects*. Geoff Rebbeck

Rebbeck, G (2016) *Heroics in e-Learning for the New Year*. Geoff Rebbeck

Redmond, P (2011, 4–7 December) *From Face-to-face Teaching to Online Teaching: Pedagogical Transitions*. Wrest Point, Hobart, Tasmania, Australia

Scott, D (2014, 1 December) *Developing a Learning Technologist*. [online] Available at: http://danielscott86.blogspot.com/2014/12/developing-learning-technologist.html (accessed 11 June 2018).

Scott, D (2015, 10 September) *Confessions of a Learning Technologist*. [online] Available at: http://danielscott86.blogspot.com/2015/09/confessions-of-learning-technologist.html (accessed 11 June 2018).

Scott, D (2016, 3 May) *A Structure of a Blended Course*. [online] Available at: http://danielscott86.blogspot.com/2016/05/a-structure-of-blended-course.html (accessed 11 June 2018).

Scott, D (2016, 3 May) *Etivities for Blended, Flip or Distance Learning*. [online] Available at: http://danielscott86.blogspot.com/2016/05/etivities-for-blended-flip-or-distance.html (accessed 11 June 2018).

Scott, D (2016, 9 May) *Smarter Learning Delivery with Digital Technology*. [online] Available at: http://danielscott86.blogspot.com/2016/05/smarter-learning-delivery-with-digital-technology.html (accessed 11 June 2018).

Scott, D (2016, 14 November) *This is proACTivity*. [online] Available at: danielscott86.blogspot.com/2016/11/this-is-proactivity.html (accessed 11 June 2018).

Scott, D (2017, 22 February) *New Course Design for Reflective Learning*. [online] Available at: http://danielscott86.blogspot.com/2017/02/new-course-design-for-reflective-learning.html (accessed 11 June 2018).

Scott, D (2017, 8 March) *Conquering Learning Design*. [online] Available at: http://danielscott86.blogspot.com/2017/03/conquering-learning-design.html (accessed 11 June 2018).

Scott, D (2017, 23 May) *Blended Learning Essentials – A Summary of Curation*. [online] Available at: http://danielscott86.blogspot.com/2017/05/blended-learning-essentials-a-summary-of-curation.html (accessed 11 June 2018).

The eLearning Coach (nd) *What Instructional Designers Do: Is This a Career for You?* [online] Available at: http://theelearningcoach.com/elearning_design/is-this-instructional-design (accessed 11 June 2018).

Useful websites

» Adobe eLearning Community – https://elearning.adobe.com

» Ann Gravells – e-learning & digital skills – www.anngravells.com/reading-lists/e-learning

» Articulate E-Learning Heroes Community – https://community.articulate.com

» BBC Active – Why you should use a Virtual Learning Environment – www.bbcactive.com/BBCActiveIdeasandResources/WhyyoushoulduseaVirtualLearningEnvironment.aspx

» Cammy Bean's Learning Visions – http://cammybean.kineo.com

» Donald Clark – Online learning design – http://planblearning.com/articles/online-learning-design

» Edinburgh Napier University – Benchmark for the use of technology in modules – http://staff.napier.ac.uk/services/vice-principal-academic/academic/TEL/TechBenchmark/Pages/Introduction.aspx

» eLearning Feeds – http://elearningfeeds.com

» eLearning Industry – https://elearningindustry.com

» Gagné's Nine Events of Instruction by Montse – http://elearningdesigner.com/storyline/gagnes-nine-events/index.html

» Gagné's Nine Events of Instruction, summary by NIU – www.niu.edu/facdev/_pdf/guide/learning/gagnes_nine_events_instruction.pdf

» infed.org – infed.org

» Instructional Design – www.instructionaldesign.org

» Jisc – Gamification and game-based learning – www.jisc.ac.uk/guides/curriculum-design-and-support-for-online-learning/gamification

» Jisc – Mobile learning – www.jisc.ac.uk/guides/mobile-learning

» Jisc – Handbook: Viewpoints for student-staff partnerships – http://repository.jisc.ac.uk/6111/1/jisc-viewpoints-handbook.pdf

- » Learning design – Not just another buzzword! – Part 1 – http://blog.ascilite.org/learning-design-not-just-another-buzzword-part-1

- » Learning design – Not just another buzzword! – Part 2 – http://blog.ascilite.org/learning-design-not-just-another-buzzword-part-2

- » Open University – How to make an open online course – www.open.edu/openlearncreate/course/view.php?id=2221

- » Open University – Innovating pedagogy – www.open.ac.uk/blogs/innovating

- » Open University – Mobilising academic content online – www.open.ac.uk/blogs/macon/toolkit

- » Open University Learning Design Initiative (OULDI) – www.open.ac.uk/blogs/OULDI

- » Open University Learning Design Initiative (OULDI) – Learning Design Toolbox – https://tinyurl.com/y7cejbme

- » Teacher Toolkit – The 5 Minute Lesson Plan – www.teachertoolkit.co.uk/the-5-minute-lesson-plan

- » The Rapid E-Learning Blog – https://blogs.articulate.com/rapid-elearning

- » University of Leicester – The 7Cs of Learning Design Toolkit – www2.le.ac.uk/projects/oer/oers/beyond-distance-research-alliance/7Cs-toolkit

- » University of York – York TEL Handbook – https://elearningyork.wordpress.com/learning-design-and-development/technology-enhanced-learning-handbook

Chapter 3 Deliver and facilitate

Chapter content

This chapter covers the following topics:

» safe practice of ILT including false knowledge;

» enabling successful delivery with ILT including technicalities, Display, Engage, Participation model, the LearningWheel and ILT in employability;

» eTutoring;

» accessibility and assistive technologies.

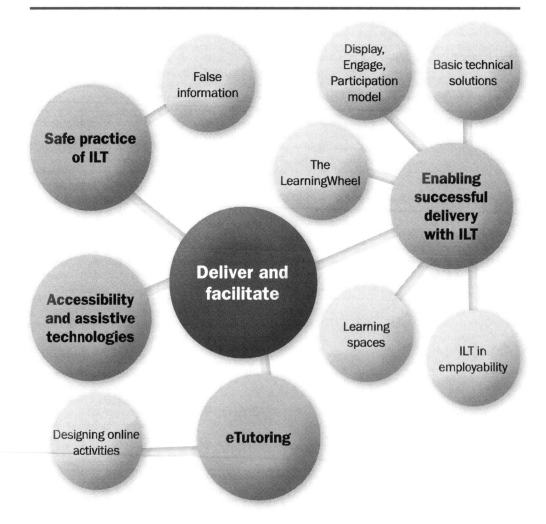

Introduction

Delivering and assessing learning with ILT is about using your classroom and available online space to connect people and integrate the personal and organisational ICT devices and tools you may use. However, a large part of using ILT successfully depends on the degree of confidence and the reliability of the networks that enable ICT systems and tools to work. Increasingly, with the growth in the use of personal devices, there are opportunities to connect devices to cloud-based platforms and resources. Whether that be using a tablet to deliver learning content in the classroom or learners interacting with an eLearning object on the VLE, it's a bit like buying a book written in a foreign language and not being able to understand it, as you don't have the skills. You and your learners will have different levels of knowledge and skills when using digital technology and the internet, perhaps due to confidence or the 'digital divide'. The digital divide is a term used to describe the national and international inequality of those who have the access and ability to use ICTs and the internet and those who don't or are restricted in some way. This can flag up potential issues and challenges when delivering and assessing learning. We have now passed a tipping point where we assume learners have access to digital technology and need to accommodate those who don't have the same access with extra help. In this chapter there will be opportunities to help you overcome or support situations like these.

Safe practice of ILT

As digital technology is readily available over the internet, it poses additional risks for you and your learners when using ILT and searching for information or communicating with others – this is termed eSafety. The following provides advice on how you can guide your learners in the safe and responsible practice of ILT and staying safe while online. It is also important to set boundaries to mitigate against situations such as learners posting unsuitable material online.

Creating a set of guidelines and ensuring that they are understood by those using ILT or an online environment can help make safety an easier process for all. It's creating ground rules if you like, just like you may have been encouraged to set for classes during your teacher education. These guidelines could be set by you, the organisation or community of interest, and should include:

» purpose/aim of use in learning, teaching and assessment;

» handling and operating;

» behaviour/netiquette;

» security;

» safety;

- » plagiarism;

- » libel;

- » confidentiality;

- » copyright;

- » General Data Protection Regulation (GDPR) – covered in Chapter 5.

In your guidelines, you may also want to include policies for general internet use; policies for using third party social media services; policies to protect younger, vulnerable learners. For example, when considering guidelines on storage you may want to mention access permissions and restrictions. Guidance on precautions should include ensuring the personal security and privacy of personal information. And it should address legal constraints; downloading of software and other digital content and inappropriate online behaviour.

When these guidelines have been established you need to consider ways you can communicate and promote them for use by others. This could be as simple as posting them on walls in your classroom. They could also be shared in your VLE and on relevant social media platforms. Make sure you keep the guidelines visible at all times and keep referring back to them. See the websites at the end of this chapter for ideas and further information on creating guidelines.

As social media is an increasingly popular tool for learning and communication, ensure that your guidelines clearly explain why and how learners need to be responsible in their use of social media and possible consequences of irresponsible actions. The following short video illustrates the importance of taking your social media footprint seriously.

Example

- » View this video that features an individual attending an interview and finding her social media footprint has unexpected consequences: https://tinyurl.com/hgj42kv

- » The message here is to keep your personal accounts set to private and use a professional account that is public. Plus, if you wouldn't say/express something face-to-face, don't be tempted to post it online. The content may be there permanently and you should never assume that private posts and messages will remain so.

» Create and implement guidelines for good practice in working with your selected ILT.

» Communicate and implement safe practice in the use of ILT to your learners.

False information

As the internet is easily accessible, so are services to create content. When we read blogs and wikis, we usually presume the information is true. It's quite an effort to check the authenticity of information and cross-reference it with other sources. Most blogs and wikis are not verified by professional bodies and these pose a high risk of readers consuming false information. The unregulated reliability and validity of web-based content can lead to false knowledge, but you can prepare your learners to learn how to judge and filter online information and assess its validity. Acknowledging the 'false news' epidemic is important not only for your learners but yourself too. Below are some tips on how you can check the authenticity of web-based content.

» Read and share the information only if you feel the source is credible enough.

» Be aware of trolls. Some people take pleasure in putting out misinformation and malicious comments to provoke others into anger or to create intentional negative reactions.

» Avoid being drawn by unrealistic and catchy headlines. It's usually 'clickbait' to gain more views to their websites. If information looks and sounds unlikely, it probably is. Be suspicious but in moderation.

» Investigate the source of the information. How valid and reliable are they? What is their reputation for accuracy like? Do they have a background in that subject that allows authenticity? Are they experts and qualified in this area? What organisations are they attached to? Check the language, spelling, punctuation and grammar they use – if there are basic spelling and grammar errors they are unlikely to be professional.

» Look at the website address/Uniform Resource Locator (URL) closely to see if it matches or belongs to the same company purporting to have published the information. A fake web page could be an excellent clone of the real web page but the URL will give away its identity.

» Review the images used. They might look authentic but if you look closely they could be manipulated or doctored and be taken out of context. Search for the image elsewhere online to check its authenticity.

» Check the dates and reporting of the information. It could be old and reused information or the actual event might be out of timeline. If similar information is not being reported by other trusted sources then it's probably unauthentic and unreliable.

» Distinguish if the information is intended for humour. Again check if the source is a known parody or comedy establishment/personality; it might just be for fun – like April Fools' Day in the United Kingdom.

Practical Task

» Identify ways to promote trust with online identities and information and how to check on them.

» Create and implement guidelines for checking on online identities and information.

Enabling successful delivery with ILT

Enabling successful delivery with ILT depends mainly on your digital capabilities, the availability of ILT you have, and the organisational boundaries and/or limitations of ICT networks. Implementing effective ILT solutions should meet the following aspects of learning, teaching, assessment and quality assurance:

» Improves efficiency and effectiveness of teaching and assessing practice generally.

» Develops innovative teaching practice with and through the use of digital technology.

» Improves staff and learner digital capabilities.

» Improves assessment and feedback practice.

» Assists in consistency and standardisation across different programmes/modules/subjects.

» Supports learner employability.

» Makes learning more fun and engaging.

As with all ILT, it is extremely important to enable as much human interaction as possible. For example, if you were participating in an online programme and had little or no introductory videos or social discussions, how would it affect your learning experience? Digital technology has had its advances; however, as humans we still need face-to-face interaction as we need to understand the emotions and behaviours of others. This is another reason why blended learning is highly desirable.

Practical Task

To help you prepare for the use of ILT in your role, use the following checklist to help you think of the things you need to plan for and set up.

☐ Select at least one digital technology device, online tool and resource to deliver or assess with. You may want to refer back to Chapter 2 to review available digital technologies.

☐ Check if the device/kit needs internet access.

☐ Charge the device/kit beforehand or have back-up supplies.

☐ Determine and identify the ways you could integrate ILT within your role for a range of purposes and tasks.

☐ Identify and create necessary accounts for using the digital technology.

☐ Decide and enable the levels of responsibility (permissions and roles) on the digital technology for participation and decide how you will manage this.

☐ Create a safe and secure environment for learning, including content to be used and/or the user interface and the work environment.

☐ Check that your digital technology is connected and accessible and set and adjust any hardware or web browser settings, ready to be used by learners.

☐ Check how you will manage learners' contributions and facilitate roles/responsibilities during the activity/task with your technology.

☐ Decide how you will respond to potential risks and resolve compatibility and access problems – see the following section.

☐ Decide and enable any archive options to save contributions made by learners that you can potentially use in future activities and tasks.

☐ Check the reality of your plans with a colleague or a learning technologist as suggested at the end of Chapter 2.

Basic technical solutions

When using various online sites and services, you will at some point inevitably experience access and compatibility issues. You may be fortunate enough to have an ICT support team or individual in your organisation; however, you can identify and resolve many of these issues if you know what to look for.

If it is an access issue, the website or service won't let you visit or log in to it. Access issues can often be traced back to the website or service server, broadband speed and capacity of your organisation/home, or down to the firewall on your computer or device. If it's an issue with broadband speed and capacity you need to contact your internet provider. If it's down to the website or service owner, then you need to contact them by telephone.

If it is a compatibility issue, the website or service will look different. The browser may even tell you that it is not viewable and/or you need to upgrade to a newer version. To resolve compatibility issues, the best way is to test the website or service thoroughly on the computer or devices and a range of platforms and browsers you may use, well before you intend on using it. This ensures the reliability and portability of using ILT across different computers, devices and browsers.

Always have a back-up plan for if your chosen digital technology does fail to operate as it should. This could include having charged devices ready to use, another choice of digital technology or going back to basics with paper-based copies of handouts and activities.

Display, Engage, Participation model

When teaching, it's important to identify what must be taught and what ought to be independently learned, without being too passive. When using any kind of ILT it is good to stop and consider the intended learning outcome and whether ILT will enhance this. ILT is sometimes used just for the sake of it without any underpinning educational purpose. For example, are you delivering active learning with ILT or through it? Take a tip from your early teacher education and focus on what you need the learner to do. Figure 3.1, The Display, Engage, Participation (DEP) model, is a good way to instantly check the purpose of what you are aiming to do.

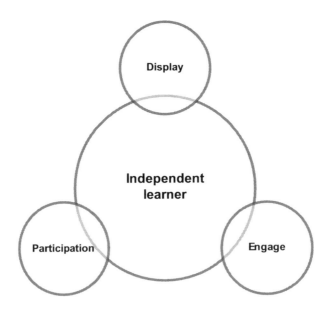

Figure 3.1. The Display, Engage, Participation model (Scott, 2014) that illustrates ways to deliver through ILT.

Display: Learners are expected to view documents, online information, videos or other media. Display is mostly concerned with rote learning where information is being conveyed but not being applied in new situations by the learner. Display considers visual principles that are applied to develop interest cues for learners. These can be in the form of context-related and accessible images, videos and animation as well as text and documents. You will define the information to be displayed before deciding on applying the visual cues. Inspiration can be drawn from graphics, visual and verbal communication to clarify presentation ideas.

Engage: Learners are expected to take information and become familiar with it but may not yet fully understand it. Learners review information from Display but re-purpose the content without fully exploring the breadth and depth of it. Engage relies heavily on interaction principles where a mutually coherent message must be sent to and from individuals to create and fulfil a feedback loop. This can be between learner and tutor but should also include interaction across the class.

Participation: Expects learners to learn independently and actively create content by applying their own understanding. Participation requires learners to be self-motivated in using information to create their own conceptual understandings. Participation is built upon collaborative characteristics; being involved with others in the process of constructing knowledge.

Practical Task

» In your VLE, instead of providing learners with multiple Microsoft Word, PDF or Microsoft PowerPoint type documents that create a long scrolling list of resources, consolidate the key bits of information into an interactive self-paced activity such as an eBook or online lesson using tools like Tes Teach (www.tes.com/lessons), iTunes U www.apple.com/education/itunes-u) or Nearpod (https://nearpod.com). You may even want to reformat your information into questions and place them in an online forum.

The LearningWheel

The LearningWheel is a learning design activity where you align your learning, teaching and assessment activities to four modes of engagement: learning content, assessment, communication and collaboration. For each of these four modes you are invited to generate a visual representation of your ideas on how you can use ILT in each mode, described as 'spokes'. The four modes are highly useful when planning for the use of ILT.

Practical Task

» Before using the LearningWheel, select any ILT tools and systems introduced in the previous chapters which are relevant to your practice and organise them according to the spokes on the LearningWheel.

» Access the LearningWheel website (https://learningwheel.co.uk).

- Create a LearningWheel account

- Review other people's collections on the website.

- A LearningWheel you may like to bookmark is Education and Training (https://learningwheel. co.uk/livewheel/education-training).

- Search on topics such as social media, VLEs, assistive technology to find relevant LearningWheels.

- Take note of the ideas, methods and ILT that people have described on the spokes.

- Create your own LearningWheel and add ideas on how you can use a variety of digital technologies you have come across.

- Share your LearningWheel on social media or a link with your colleagues to gain further ideas and feedback.

To learn about new and innovative pedagogies to use through ILT, visit the Open University's Innovating Pedagogy (www.open.ac.uk/blogs/innovating).

Learning spaces

A 'learning space' could be a face-to-face environment within a quiet corner of your organisation's library, or some comfortable seating that has been placed near a coffee area. It may be virtual space such as an online group chat which learners have set up. A good approach to encourage blended learning is by using a learning space flexibly, and increasing personalisation by encouraging learners to use their personal devices in their learning. In doing so this may promote greater engagement and allow learners some choice in their own learning. As with the flipped learning approach, you may want to encourage your learners to be more self-reliant and work outside of the classroom on a project or assignment. Flipped learning helps break down some of the barriers and confinement that are created by the classroom walls. You could allow learners to work together in groups in a format of their choice, such as an online group/environment or in an agreed area in the establishment, like the library. For group and project management tasks, it may be helpful to use collaboration tools like Trello (https://trello.com) and

Microsoft OneNote or Teams via Office 365 (www.office.com). These tools are good for capturing conversations and shared resources, which may be more efficient than sending multiple emails. You can then oversee the activity and dip in where you feel you need to.

Practical Task

» Review Appendix 3.1 that contains a summary of practical ways you can use ILT in your practices – this is not an exhaustive list. Are there any areas of your practice that you think are missing from the list? If so, what ideas do you have? Who can help you make them happen?

» If you already use digital technology in this way, reflect on what else you could do to make this experience better for your learners. How can your learners contribute to the planning and design of this process?

» Critically analyse where and how you can use ILT as a means of embedding and promoting English and maths in your schemes of work, learning programme and lessons. There is a useful resource 'Embedding English and Maths: Practical Strategies' in the 'References and further reading' section.

Reflective Task

The issues in Table 3.1 may highlight common ILT issues in your role. Review the possible solutions suggested and reflect on how you can use these and/or extend them further in your practices.

Table 3.1. Potential ILT issues you may encounter.

Issue	Possible solution	Ideas
Making better use of class time		
Are there any parts of your programme where class time is used inefficiently (for example, taking notes from Microsoft PowerPoint presentations)?	Put your existing learning and teaching materials online. Learners can access them in their own time, then class time is used for more discussions and collaborative work.	

Issue	Possible solution	Ideas
Are parts of your programme delivered with little variety of online learning activities and resources?	Ask your learners about the variety you provide them with. Create a range of online activities and resources using your VLE or other tools and refer to these regularly so that your learners know they are core to the programme.	
Are there parts of the programme where you spend lots of time saying similar things to different individuals?	Enable your online learning materials on the VLE or other tools to confirm when a learner has accessed or participated in them.	
Are there parts of the programme where you spend a lot of class time practising the same points?	Use a variety of OERs and online environments that will allow learners to practise the key ideas at their own pace and level.	
Creating more interesting learning materials		
Are many of your teaching handouts text heavy?	Use Google search or other sites mentioned to find related pictures and icons or you could use a mobile phone or your organisation's video camera.	
Are many of your handouts static/passive Word or PDF documents?	Use functions in your VLE or other tools to consolidate the text into bitesize chunks of information. Include pictures to make it more appealing.	
Do your learning materials lack differentiation?	Using your VLE or other system, create conditional learning resources that are unlocked when certain criteria are met.	

Issue	Possible solution	Ideas
Teaching/assessing difficult concepts		
Are there concepts that are difficult for your learners to understand?	Link from various words or definitions on your VLE or other tools to a glossary or other web-based resources, including images and videos.	
Are there any processes that are difficult to visualise?	Create visual presentations using Prezi (https://prezi.com) or Popplet (http://popplet.com) for example. Or even videos that allow learners to replay or pause as many times as they want.	
Are learners unclear about assessment requirements?	Create online interactive tasks where learners view weak answers that enable learners to build up to strong answers.	

ILT in employability

Employability is about individuals developing knowledge, skills and personal attributes in order to successfully gain employment. Employability skills should be encouraged and embedded throughout learning programmes, like functional skills are.

Qualification specifications provide a list of criteria where learners are required to demonstrate subject-specific knowledge and performance or competence, which are referred to as hard skills. Soft skills are aspects that distinguish one learner from another, which could be referred to as 'personability'. Examples include imagination, reflection, adaptability, empathy and sociability. Soft skills which define our character are not taught but can be developed through taking part in activities on campus or in the classroom.

Soft skills are often not captured or included in lessons as they may not directly meet qualification criteria. This is a potential problem when learners start seeking employment. Employers are keen to see the soft skills demonstrated by the candidate as this helps them gauge how well they would fit into the job role and interact with customers. Soft skills are often assessed in the interview, which typically provides only one chance at making a favourable impression! A range of soft skills can be captured in an ePortfolio that demonstrates how learners work, work with others, share, support others, conduct enquiry, demonstrate curiosity and so forth. In short, everything that takes our learners from college or adult learning to a work-ready mindset.

Social media can be used to help your learners stand out from the crowd to enhance their employability as well as their learning. Everything we create and do online leaves a trail of our online identity; this is called a digital footprint. A digital footprint can be used positively when looking for new jobs or promoting yourself. Potential employers may search for information on candidates, so make sure you put out the information you want them to find. Make your information as accurate, positive and influential as possible.

LinkedIn (www.linkedin.com) is a popular platform for connecting and networking with other professionals and employers. It is a great example of how to create and manage a professional digital identity. You can use your LinkedIn profile as an online CV to increase your searchability and discoverability among other professionals. You can look for jobs or may be lucky enough to be headhunted as employers come across your profile. You can join groups to collaborate and publish pieces of work to showcase your knowledge, skills and experience.

Practical Task

» Before commencing this task, ensure that you and your learners are comfortable with:

- using search engines like Google and Bing;
- job searching;
- creating and managing digital identity and footprint;
- managing privacy and visibility;
- considering General Data Protection Regulation (GDPR).

» Enable and encourage your learners to create a professional profile on LinkedIn or an ePortfolio using something like Blogger (www.blogger.com) to increase their searchability and discoverability, by showcasing their knowledge, skills and personal attributes through project work they have done.

» Creating a professional profile or ePortfolio like this will allow employers to view material before they are invited to interview, which can help when employers shortlist. Online presence also:

- enables discussion points during the interview;
- demonstrates knowledge, practical skills and creative thinking;
- demonstrates personality and likability, which may be equally important to skills and knowledge.

eTutoring

eTutoring is another way of saying online tutoring. It is where you deliver and facilitate learning within an online environment, usually to support learners in blended and distance-learning situations. The eTutoring role begins by initiating a learning activity, facilitating and motivating learners as they work on it to right through to giving feedback and assessment. It's a similar approach you already use in face-to-face situations.

The increasing abundance of online tools and resources may have challenged you to use more flexible and diverse ranges of digital technologies to meet the needs and demands of today's learners. This may have resulted in you needing training to help you facilitate and manage learning within these rapidly evolving and dynamic online learning environments.

Like all good lessons and assessments, eTutorials needs well-thought-out planning and preparation. Figure 3.2, the Five-Stage Model, describes how learners typically engage with others online and helps eTutors to promote scaffolding, engagement and building confidence for their learners. As with face-to-face delivery, in online environments it is good practice to have a plan of activities, roles and responsibilities to avoid miscommunication and confusion for learners. Table 3.2 describes briefly the principles behind the Five-Stage Model to help you introduce and facilitate online discussions and other activities. You may even want to use this model as a way to introduce ILT to your learners at an appropriate level. Your learners will appreciate the support and encouragement during any use of online learning and ILT. The model also offers a developmental process to support you in building your confidence and skills in online learning.

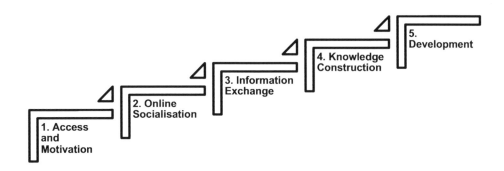

Figure 3.2. The stages to introducing learners online and facilitating and developing their learning through the Five-Stage Model. The amount of participation/interaction from learners that you can anticipate increases through stages 1–4 and then tends to reduce at stage 5.

Adapted from Salmon (2011)

Table 3.2. Descriptions of the Five-Stage Model.

Stage	Description	eTutor activity
Access and motivation	The overall aim is to promote and encourage learners to access regularly and share work to increase participation. Learners may have difficulty in accessing and navigating with digital technology, which can be demotivating for learning activities. This could be due to learners' ICT skills and familiarity with the technology used. Guidance and instruction from you on the activity can provide fundamental and motivational support.	• Setting up, introducing and accessing system • Site navigation – where to go and what to find • Welcome and encouragement • Outline purpose and tasks • Guidance on where to find technical support
Online socialisation	Learners are making connections to others in terms of knowing who has similar interests, knowledge and skills in different areas. They are working together on common tasks. However, not all learners may want to participate or contribute. This can be a challenge to get learners to participate together; if this is not done promptly, it may appear to learners that the activity is unsuccessful or inactive and therefore demotivating. Icebreakers can be used at the start of any activity. However, be aware of any netiquette issues as they can also result in barriers to communication and motivation.	• Introductions • Icebreakers • Ground rules • Netiquette/guidelines • Enable and promote socialisation

Stage	Description	eTutor activity
Information exchange	Learners are independently sharing work and responding to feedback without prompts. They are appreciating the information that is available in the learning environment. If learners are not motivated and engaged at this stage, they will find it hard to participate and contribute information. Learners will need to know how to respond and critique others on their knowledge and contributions for successful learning development. Effective facilitation, feedback and moderation can reduce risk here.	• High preparation and planning • Facilitate structured activities • Assign roles and responsibilities • Support use of learning materials • Encourage discussions • Introduce feedback
Knowledge construction	You as an eTutor are highly active at this point in facilitating and encouraging peer review and feedback. The eTutor gives constructive feedback and relates it to concepts and theories. Learners need to be interacting with your content at this stage. This stage highly depends on social participation and contributions of programme content for knowledge construction to occur.	• High tutor involvement • Facilitate open activities • Facilitate the process • Asking questions (start to expose critical thinking) • Encourage reflection • Weave – pull together learners' contributions and connect them to other learners and link to your programme material • Summarise – with a long discussion or collaborative activity, provide a summary of what happened and quote comments or responses from learners

Stage	Description	eTutor activity
Development	Learners become responsible for their own learning with little support from the eTutor. However, the eTutor can share resources for further skills development for their own needs and desires to improve. Learners will demonstrate criticality, confidence and reflection in both their own and other's contributions and the use of the digital technology. Learners should now be expressing independence and showing clarity in their understanding.	• Tutor is less active and hands over to the learners • Respond only when required • Encourage critical thinking and reflection • Pose challenging questions and arguments at this stage to encourage deeper thinking and reflection

When planning and moderating for eTutoring, there are some areas of which you need to be aware. The following lists some of these aspects for you to consider and develop strategies on how to deal with them:

Address

» Managing and monitoring dialogue of learning.

» Sustaining encouragement demands serious commitment.

» Quality contributions require discourse to be focused and productive.

» Awareness of cognitive and social presence.

» Timing of responses to be carefully considered (timetabling and maintaining momentum).

Concerns

» Time in accessing and reviewing contributions and interpreting them before responding.

» Lack of empathy and personal involvement.

» The expectation of 'leaving learners to it'.

» Asynchronous vs synchronous digital technologies.

» Some learners may not respond but it doesn't mean they are not present; this is referred to as 'positive silent engagement'. Be mindful that some learners may contribute in different ways.

Apply

» Empathise

» Motivating

» Prompting

» Challenging

» Weaving

» Summarising

Before planning and delivering online learning, you may want to check that your learners are ready to participate in online learning environments. Just as you do when you join a gym, you are recommended to undertake an assessment of your abilities to use certain equipment. Administering an 'Online Activity Readiness Questionnaire' will help you to determine your learners' motivations and interactions in an online environment for you to design and plan around. See Appendix 3.2 for an example questionnaire you could use with them.

Designing online activities

In Chapter 2, you were introduced to a learning design process, which included planning an online activity identifying what learners are expected to do and how you anticipated facilitating that process online. The online activities (Etivity) invitation template is a useful way to establish the purpose and structure of an online activity. Following the template below will allow you to think and map learning content with an appropriate on-line activity that enables participation using your chosen digital technology.

Etivity templates as shown in Figure 3.3 are a good way of making a connection and the spark to learning content. Delivering learning content online gives you the opportunity to be creative and more adventurous when linking resources to tasks. The screenshot illustrates a template you can follow, allowing you to think through the who, what, why, when, where and how of delivering an online learning task. Visit (www.gillysalmon.com/e-tivities.html) for further guidance in completing Etivity invitations.

Figure 3.4 demonstrates how the Etivity invitation has been applied to the forum feature within a VLE. The invitation was used to design the activity and instructions of what learners are expected to do, how it meets programme requirements and next steps. You can take the idea of the invitation and adapt as necessary according to the learning requirements and the ILT you have chosen to deliver it through.

Etivity invitation template	
Numbering and pacing and sequencing	Learning in the digital world (1 of 2).
Title	Learning in the digital world.
Purpose	Doing this Etivity will aid towards achieving Learning Outcomes 1.1, 1.2 and 1.3 of the unit 'Introduction to the Digital Learning Environment'.
Brief summary of overall task	This Etivity aims to discuss what is meant by 'Digital Learning Environment' and the advantages and disadvantages it poses.
Spark	www.jiscdigitalmedia.ac.uk/guide/introduction-to-the-use-of-vles-with-digital-media
Individual contribution	1. Read the article above and suggest what is a Digital Learning Environment. 2. Explain some advantages and disadvantages of using them. 3. Suggest one free and one payable Digital Learning Environment.
Dialogue begins	Please reply back to the questions above with at least one new post and at least one other post replying back to an individual with an explanation why you agree or disagree. You may post supporting links to support your contribution.
eTutor interventions	Question, quote, direct and observe the discussion.
Schedule and time	Complete your contributions by 'date and time'.
Next	Learning in the digital world (2 of 2).

Etivity invitation template	
Numbering and pacing and sequencing	Learning in the digital world (2 of 2).
Title	Learning in the digital world.
Purpose	Doing this Etivity, will aid towards achieving Learning Outcomes 4.1, 4.2 and 4.4 of the unit 'Introduction to the Digital Learning Environment'.
Brief summary of overall task	This Etivity you will evaluate the Digital Learning Environment.
Spark	http://tools.jiscinfonet.ac.uk/downloads/vle/what-is-vle.pdf
Individual contribution	1. Read the article above (page 20). 2. Taking your limitations from the first discussion (1 of 2) and focus on Moodle. What suggestions do you have that can improve Moodle? 3. What benefits does Moodle have over using traditional teaching methods?
Dialogue begins	Please reply back to the questions above with at leas t one new post and at least one other post replying back to an individual with an explanation why you agree or disagree. You may post supporting links to support your contribution.
eTutor interventions	Question, quote, direct and observe the discussion.
Schedule and time	Complete your contributions by 'date and time'.
Next	Prepare a written account using your knowledge from the two discussions and place on your ePortfolio under the page Introduction to the Digital Learning Environment.

Figure 3.3. An Etivity invitation template.
Adapted from Salmon (2013)

VLE forum topics			
Discussion	Started by	Replies	Last post
Learning in the digital world (1 of 2).	Profile picture, user name	12	User name Date and time
Learning in the digital world (2 of 2).	Profile picture, user name	21	User name Date and time

---

Profile picture	Post title: Learning in the digital world (1 of 2). By user name Date and time of post

Post content

Brief: This Etivity aims to discuss what is meant by 'Digital Learning Environment' and the advantages and disadvantages it poses.

Purpose: In doing this Etivity, it will aid towards achieving Learning Outcomes 1.1, 1.2 and 1.3 of the unit 'Introduction to the Digital Learning Environment'.

Resource: www.jiscdigitalmedia.ac.uk/guide/introduction-to-the-use-of-vles-with-digital-media

Task:

1. Read the article above and suggest what a Digital Learning Environment is.

2. Explain some advantages and disadvantages of using them.

3. Suggest one free and one payable Digital Learning Environment.

Rule: Please reply back to the questions above with at least **one new** post and at least one other post **replying back** to an individual with an explanation why you agree or disagree. You may post supporting links to support your contribution.

Deadline: Complete your contributions by 'date and time'.

Next: Learning in the digital world (2 of 2).

Edit   Delete   Reply

Profile picture	Post title: Learning in the digital world (2 of 2). By user name Date and time of post

Post content

Brief: This Etivity you will evaluate the Digital Learning Environment.

Purpose: In doing this Etivity, it will aid towards achieving Learning Outcomes 4.1, 4.2 and 4.4 of the unit 'Introduction to the Digital Learning Environment'.

Resource: http://tools.jiscinfonet.ac.uk/downloads/vle/what-is-vle.pdf

Task:

1. Read the article above (page 20).

2. Taking your limitations from the first discussion (1 of 2) and focuson Moodle. What suggestions do you have that can improve Moodle?

3. What benefits does Moodle have over using traditional teaching methods?

Rule: Please reply back to the questions above with at least **one new** post and at least one other post **replying back** to an individual with an explanation why you agree or disagree. You may post supporting links to support your contribution.

Deadline: Complete your contribution s by 'date and time'.

Next: Prepare a written account using your knowledge from the two discussions and place on your ePortfolio under the page Introduction to the Digital Learning Environment.

Edit   Delete   Reply

Figure 3.4. An online activity within a forum for learners to participate in showing how the Etivity invitation template in Figure 3.3 has been applied in a VLE forum.

Accessibility and assistive technologies

Accessibility is about ensuring everyone, especially your learners, has access to resources and services, while ensuring that it is easy for them to obtain and interact with your materials. Accessibility is about providing people with as many options as possible, not so much about providing one form or mode of access. Assistive technology means using tools, systems and devices that remove barriers to learning caused by an impairment. It is not about choosing a specific operating system or device.

To learn effectively you need to be in the right mindset and environment to fully store, recall and interact with knowledge. Due to our own preferences, when we learn in a classroom or online we may prefer a desktop or mobile device to help store knowledge and information. However, using different types of devices can either enable or hinder your process of learning. For example, you may prefer to use a laptop to have more screen space and a keyboard to focus, study and type. Mobile devices may be limiting for some people who need to use multiple windows and files to research and absorb information or find it difficult to type on screen. Using personal devices is a great way of embedding assistive technologies because it is likely already mapped to the learner's preferences. However, be prepared that some learners will not have access to personal devices or may prefer not to use their own devices on campus. Find out if you can borrow sufficient devices from your information technology department or library for the lesson or the day so that all learners can be included in any ILT-related activities.

Assistive technologies can help learners to better use digital technologies if they have a physical or learning disability or have accessibility preferences. Assistive technologies aim to increase access to learning, by improving flexibility and inclusion. In terms of ILT and eLearning, assistive technologies often include screen readers, voice recognition and screen magnification software. For example, in your VLE you may have the option to change background colour, text size and the ability to speak text aloud on the web page. You can also purchase ergonomic mice and keyboards to suit specific needs to enable greater access to digital technologies.

There is a legal obligation to make learning materials accessible, outlined in the Special Educational Needs and Disability Act (2001). Also, your employer may have specific requirements that must be followed to ensure you meet the regulatory requirements as well as your learners' needs.

Practical Task

» Select an online tool or device you are using or want to use with your learners.

» Consider the opportunities and constraints the ILT tools presents.

» Identify and assess a range of assistive and adaptive technologies to support your learners in their learning.

» Investigate the accessibility options and features that are available to help your learners use the tool or device to fully participate in the learning activity.

It is also important to consider accessibility when presenting your materials electronically. The following are some suggestions you could follow in the planning and designing of your teaching activities and resources.

» Ensure the format and layout of your materials are clear, concise and consistent. Information should be appropriately presented so that learners can navigate it easily.

» Make alternate versions of your materials available to your learners, for example, if using Microsoft PowerPoint. Make video, PDF and Microsoft Word documents available with accessibility options on, such as the 'navigation pane', to increase readability.

» Ensure that relevant software is installed on the computers and devices and that it works. This will reduce time and frustration for you and learners trying to solve these problems during the session.

» Use appropriate sans-serif fonts such as Arial and styles to increase readability.

» Choose appropriate colours: be aware of any learners that have visual impairments, don't use difficult-to-read colours like yellow, and ensure there is sufficient contrast between background colours and text.

» Ensure that any images you use have descriptions attached to them (alternative text). This will mean that the text description you've added will be read out to anyone using a screen reader.

» All diagrams and tables are labelled.

» Add descriptive text to hyperlinks, rather than saying 'click here' as the link may not be visible to some people.

The 'Accessibility Checker' feature in Microsoft applications is useful to help you identify any areas for consideration. You may want to consider the conditions that Figure 3.5 illustrates and perhaps select and implement an appropriate mix of text, images, audio, video and interactions to meet the wider needs of your learners – it's about being inclusive by design.

If you would like to gain a greater understanding of accessibility and assistive technologies, access the following links to free courses and resources.

» OpenLearn – Introduction to cyber security: Stay safe online – www.open.edu/ openlearn/science-maths-technology/introduction-cyber-security-stay-safe-online/ content-section-overview

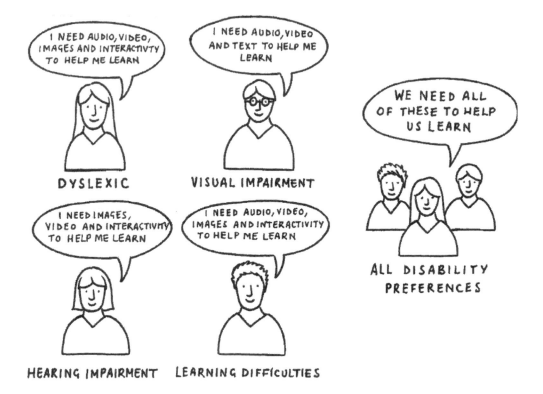

Figure 3.5. Images adapted from 'Accessibility Issues in Online Learning' webinar from Jisc's Alistair McNaught on 23 October 2015.

» OpenLearn – Accessibility of eLearning – www.open.edu/openlearn/education-development/education-careers/accessibility-elearning/content-section-0

» OpenLearn – Assistive technologies and online learning – www.open.edu/openlearn/ education-development/assistive-technologies-and-online-learning/content-section-0

» FutureLearn – Digital Accessibility: Enabling Participation in the Information Society – www.futurelearn.com/courses/digital-accessibility

For more information and guidance on using tools to create digital activities and resources while maintaining accessibility and promoting inclusivity, see Jisc's guides: www.jisc. ac.uk/guides/using-assistive-and-accessible-technology-in-teaching-and-learning and www.jisc.ac.uk/guides/meeting-the-requirements-of-learners-with-special-educational-needs or Dyslexia Action: www.dyslexiaaction.org.uk

Summary

This chapter encouraged you to develop and extend your digital practitioner skills by identifying, using and applying a wide range of digital technologies. This ranged from outlining guidelines and safe practice of ILT, preparing your digital tools and resources to facilitate learning face-to-face and online, to identifying appropriate digital technologies for learning needs. You were introduced to eTutoring; how to facilitate learning in an online environment, and explored accessibility and assistive technologies to support the needs and preferences of your learners.

References and further reading

Attwell, G and Hughes, J (2010) *Pedagogic Approaches to Using Technology for Learning – Literature Review*. London: Lifelong Learning UK.

Collis, B A and Moonen, J (2005) *An On-Going Journey: Technology as a Learning Workbench*. Enschede, the Netherlands: University of Twente.

Garrison, D R (2011) *E-Learning in the 21st Century* (2nd edition). London: Routledge.

Gravells, A (2017) *Principles and Practices of Teaching and Training: A Guide for Teachers and Trainers in the FE and Skills Sector*. London: Learning Matters.

Hopkins, D (2017) *Emergency Rations: #EdTechRations*. CreateSpace Independent Publishing Platform.

Jisc (2015, 23 October) 'Accessibility Issues in Online Learning' webinar from Jisc's Alistair McNaught.

Kellsey, D and Taylor, A (2016) *The LearningWheel: A Model of Digital Pedagogy*. Northwich: Critical Publishing Ltd.

Magid, L and Gallagher, K (2015) *The Educator's Guide to Social Media*. [online] Available at: www.connectsafely.org/wp-content/uploads/eduguide.pdf (last accessed 11 June 2018).

Petty, G (2009) *Evidence-based Teaching: A Practical Approach* (2nd edition). Cheltenham: Nelson Thornes.

Petty, G (2014) *Teaching Today: A Practical Guide* (5th edition). Oxford: Open University Press.

Salmon, G (2011) *E-Moderating: The Key to Online Teaching and Learning* (3rd edition). New York: Routledge.

Salmon, G (2013) *E-Tivities: The Key to Active Online Learning* (2nd edition). Routledge.

Scott, D (2014, 3 July) *A Little Deeper with eLearning*. [online] Available at: http://danielscott86.blogspot.com/2014/07/a-little-deeper-with-elearning.html (accessed 11 June 2018).

Scott, D (2016, 3 May) *Etivities for Blended, Flip or Distance Learning*. [online] Available at: http://danielscott86.blogspot.com/2016/05/etivities-for-blended-flip-or-distance.html (accessed 11 June 2018).

Scott, D (2016, 1 June) *An Experience of Facilitating an Online Discussion*. [online] Available at: http://danielscott86.blogspot.com/2016/06/an-experience-of-facilitating-online.html (accessed 11 June 2018).

Scott, D (2016, 31 July) *Putting Learning into Learning Technology: Developing a Pedagogical Rationale to Deliver eLearning*. [online] Available at: http://danielscott86.blogspot.com/2016/10/putting-learning-into-learning-technology-developing-a-pedagogical-rationale-to-deliver-eLearning.html (accessed 11 June 2018).

Scott, D (2017, 23 February) *Display, Engage, Participation*. [online] Available at: http://danielscott86.blogspot.com/2017/02/display-engage-participation.html (accessed 11 June 2018).

Scott, D (2017, 4 May) *Digital Inauthenticity – The Rising Epidemic*. [online] Available at: http://danielscott86.blogspot.com/2017/05/digital-inauthenticity-the-rising-epidemic.html (accessed 11 June 2018).

Scott, D (2017, 30 May) *eTutoring – Models for Facilitating Online Discussions*. [online] Available at: http://danielscott86.blogspot.com/2017/05/etutoring-models-for-facilitating.html (accessed 11 June 2018).

Scott, D (2018, 3 August) *Why openness is good*. http://danielscott86.blogspot.com/2018/08/why-openness-is-good.html (accessed 11 June 2018).

Scruton, J and Ferguson, B (2014) *Teaching and Supporting Adult Learners*. Northwich: Critical Publishing Ltd.

Sharrock, T (2016) *Embedding English and Maths: Practical Strategies for FE and Post-16 Tutors*. Northwich: Critical Publishing Ltd.

Siemens, G (2004) *Connectivism: A Learning Theory for the Digital Age*. Elearnspace. [online] Available at: www.elearnspace.org/Articles/connectivism.htm (last accessed 11 June 2018).

Wenger-Trayner, B and Wenger-Trayner, E (2015) *Introduction to Communities of practice: A Brief Overview of the Concept and Its Use*. [online] Available at: http://wenger-trayner.com/introduction-to-communities-of-practice (accessed 11 June 2018).

Yacci, M (2000) Interactivity Demystified: A Structural Definition for Distance Education and Intelligent CBT. *Educational Technology*, 40(4): 5–16.

Useful websites

» BBC accessibility standards and guidelines – www.bbc.co.uk/accessibility/best_practice/standards.shtml

» BBC WebWise – Top 10 online safety tips – www.bbc.co.uk/webwise/0/21259413

» Childline – Staying safe online – www.childline.org.uk/info-advice/bullying-abuse-safety/online-mobile-safety/staying-safe-online

» Gilly Salmon – E-Moderating introduction – www.gillysalmon.com/e-moderating.html

» Get Safe Online – www.getsafeonline.org

» Gov.uk – Dos and don'ts on designing for accessibility – https://accessibility.blog.gov.uk/2016/09/02/dos-and-donts-on-designing-for-accessibility

» Jisc – Technology for employability toolkit – http://ji.sc/tech_for_employ_toolkit

» NSPCC – Online safety – www.nspcc.org.uk/preventing-abuse/keeping-children-safe/online-safety

» Safety Net Kids – Staying safe online – www.safetynetkids.org.uk/personal-safety/staying-safe-online

» UK Safer Internet Centre – www.saferinternet.org.uk

Chapter 4 Assess

Chapter content

This chapter covers the following topics:

» eAssessment, including considerations for eAssessment;

» designing for eAssessment, including assessment planning, assessment activity, collecting work-based evidence, assessment decisions and giving feedback and ePortfolios;

» ILT in quality assurance.

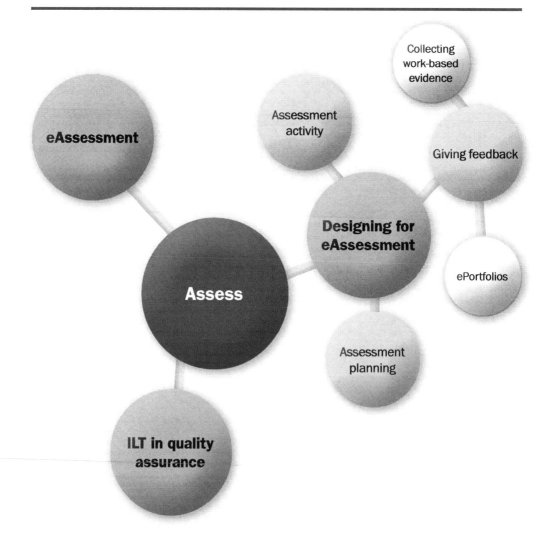

Introduction

Traditional paper-based evidence is often now presented visually and digitally instead. So your assessment practices may need to change to accommodate this. Learning technology can invigorate your assessment as well as your teaching. It is more interesting to assess and give feedback on an ePortfolio full of rich multimedia rather than a traditional document. However, this depends on how much time you invest in designing digital assessments. This is a good area to make a start in rethinking your current assessment practices and moving from traditional to inspirational.

eAssessment

There are interchangeable definitions of eAssessment such as computer-based or computer-assisted assessment; however, they all mean the same thing. eAssessment covers all kinds of digital technologies that are used to assist assessment and feedback. Overall, eAssessment increases the interactivity and productivity of assessment design and practice and providing and accessing feedback, for example:

» Enables and captures breadth and depth of knowledge, skills and experiences that may not be easily assessed by other methods.

» Benefits learners who may have difficulties with traditional forms of assessment due to distance, disability, illness, or work commitments.

» Increases choice and flexibility in the method, timing and location of assessment.

» Reduces marking time and the need for paper-based assessments.

» Provides instant individual and adaptive feedback.

» Increases learner engagement of their feedback.

» Improves administration and quality assurance processes.

As a result it enhances the core principles of assessment, which are:

» Valid – relevant to the assessment criteria.

» Authentic – produced by the learner.

» Current – relevant to the time of assessment.

» Sufficient – satisfies the assessment criteria.

» Reliable – consistent across the qualification/subject and at the required level.

Designing for eAssessment

Designing for eAssessment should start with your programme specification: the curriculum. In Chapter 2 the DADDIE model was introduced to help define learning requirements. Designing both formative and summative assessment first is a good way of establishing the learning requirements. Consider whether the assessment can be digitally enabled or not, and align it to the learning requirements, curriculum content, learner needs and underpinning pedagogy.

Assessment is most successful when learning and teaching activities are aligned to the learning requirements and curriculum to be taught. Understanding clearly articulated programme requirements will allow you to develop a range of assessment opportunities for your learners to demonstrate their knowledge, skills and competence within the curriculum.

Assessment planning

Assessment and feedback have a cycle of their own: planning the assessment, creating it, supporting learners during the assessment, learners submitting their work, providing feedback and grades to learners, learners receiving feedback, the tutor reflecting on the process and the learner reflecting on their feedback to identify areas for improvement.

Diagnostic assessment is the first stage of assessing your learner's knowledge and skills before they begin a programme. Your organisation may have bespoke systems that allow your learners to undertake a diagnostic assessment to capture their Functional Skills levels in English, maths and ICT. You may have access to your learners' personal details on tutorial systems or dashboards that list their entry qualifications and experience as well as any specific requirements they have. However, you may want to establish your learners' current skills and experiences with digital technology, so that you can plan more precisely when embedding ILT effectively into your lessons and build your learners' digital capabilities in the process. You may like to revisit Chapter 1 to determine your learners' digital capabilities using the Online Learning Readiness Tool and the online activity readiness questionnaire in Chapter 3. It's useful to find out what digital skills and technologies your learners have and are using, and how confident they are in deploying these skills, as it will help you to encourage learners to be independent when collecting their evidence using digital technologies.

Assessment activity

Much of your assessment activity may centre around checking learning and giving formative and informative feedback, which is assessment for learning.

» Review Table 4.1, which lists some ways of using popular eAssessment tools that may be available in your organisation. These will enable you to use various ways of checking and testing learning and providing feedback.

» Which of the eAssessment tools listed in Table 4.1 do you have access to and could explore further in your practices?

Table 4.1. Describing ways to use eAssessment tools.

Digital technology	Activity
Audio feedback	Providing audio feedback to learners enhances communication by revealing the tone of voice often invisible in text-based feedback and removes the problem of illegible handwriting. It enables learners to listen to all feedback and not pick and choose aspects of it, which can increase their motivation in taking it on board.
Assignments	Document upload tools such as Dropbox (www.dropbox.com) and similar features can be found in a VLE. These allow learners to upload files for you to check and assess. This gives learners more flexibility over when and what they choose to share with you.
Blogs	Allowing learners to create their own or having a blog space within the VLE will enable them to write about their learning on an ongoing basis. This increases reflection and personalisation of what they are learning and how they intend on using it. You can add comments and encourage learners to share their posts with others for peer feedback.
Conditional activity release	Many VLEs have a function where you can restrict activities or assessments that only become available after meeting specific criteria. For example, you may want your learners to achieve at least 50 per cent in a quiz before accessing the next learning activity. Learners must achieve 50 per cent in order to see and participate in the next resource. This is a good way to enable differentiated learning resources for learners at different levels.

Digital technology	Activity
eLearning objects	Creating specific bespoke interactive eLearning materials will allow you to align your learning content, assessment requirements and feedback directly to your programme curriculum. This could be a lengthy process if the volume of content is large.
Interactive whiteboard	You can insert worksheets or handouts and open them up to individuals, the class or split learners into groups and ask them to annotate and contribute answers to the board.
Mobile devices	Many online sites and tools now have app versions or mobile-enabled web pages. This increases the accessibility of these digital technologies where learners can take pictures or recordings and upload them directly to the site. Or learners may be able to upload directly to the VLE or upload their assignment directly.
Online forums	You can use forums for online learning activities and as a communication tool with your learners. Learners can be given topics to discuss and work together on that generate evidence that could be later used in ePortfolios. Forums can enable peer feedback and collaboration to support knowledge as well as building ideas for a learner's own assessment. They are a practical way to give informative feedback on conversations that occur online.
Peer assessment	In a VLE, you can create activities that allow learners to submit a piece of work which is automatically assigned to another learner for review. Other tools like Turnitin (http://turnitinuk.com), which allow work to be uploaded, marked and checked for plagiarism, offer this feature on submitted pieces of work. Additionally, through peer assessment you can make learning a more social experience.
Polling devices	Using learners' own mobile phones or clicker devices, you can check class learning through open, closed or critical questioning – both tutor or student led. Results are instant and can be downloaded for evidence or to show to an awarding organisation. • Kahoot! – https://kahoot.com • Mentimeter – www.mentimeter.com • Microsoft Forms – https://forms.office.com • Plickers – www.plickers.com • Poll Everywhere – www.polleverywhere.com • Quizlet – https://quizlet.com • Socrative – www.socrative.com

Digital technology	Activity
	Be mindful not to exclude learners who don't have access to the internet or mobile device; perhaps pair them up with someone. Also, some learners may have limited text/data allowances.
Recording devices/lecture capture	Learners can record practical activities to demonstrate that they are carrying out various tasks to meet programme criteria. Video is very powerful as it clearly shows that learners are demonstrating that competency. You can be there in person to record these or learners can record themselves and send you the video to assess. However, ensure you get written consent from any customers or clients who may be in the video and keep the file safe, conforming to confidentiality regulations.
Screencast feedback	When giving learners feedback, you can open up their work on your computer, record yourself and talk through briefly what you are assessing. This might not be used to give summative feedback, but as a short introduction to give a personal element to it.
Self-assessment quizzes with instant and adaptive feedback	Many VLEs offer in-built quiz tools that allow you to use a variety of question types such as drag and drop, matching, essay, numerical, multiple choice, fill in the blank, either/or, true or false, and even branching. You could use them for: • pre-learning questionnaire; • quiz based on case studies; • scenario/role-play based quiz; • end of lesson/workshop quiz to consolidate learning; • weekly/topical quiz to summarise learning; • post-learning/self-evaluation questionnaire; • exam/test readiness quiz. These quizzes can be graded or ungraded depending on assessment preferences. There are websites such as H5P (https://h5p.org) assessments or Tes Teach (www.tes.com/lessons) where you can create and embed a quiz in your VLE or own site. Vary and change your question design to avoid being predicable and guessable as this could result in low levels of challenge. Depending on your choice of digital technology, eAssessment activities can often generate automatic feedback depending on what has been answered – which is useful for adaptive feedback.
Simulations and games	Using simulations or games is an interesting and fun way to assess learners. While some can be very informal, they increase engagement and motivation. Access the websites at the end of this chapter for suggested tools or you can search for more using the internet.

Giving feedback

At the summative stage for assessment of learning, you may be using online submission tools such as a VLE assignment upload, Dropbox and Turnitin tools. Often, assignment upload tools will allow you to leave short or long comments and have options for leaving audio and annotated feedback. Annotated feedback is where you can leave interactive place markers such as question marks, ticks and crosses. These are good for drawing learners to your comments for them to act upon. You may even be able to grade work using criteria you have set.

Additionally, you may have the added bonus of having a plagiarism detector (Turnitin offers this feature). Once a piece of work is submitted, the plagiarism software will scan the text for any similarities against other people's work nationally and internationally who have submitted through that system. Systems like these can also annotate the text to show where text may have been copied from the original source. This is ideal to prompt a discussion with your learners about plagiarism and originality, and for you to decide the best course of action.

Online submission tools are ideal for providing final feedback on assignment or project work as you can leave overall comments on the collection over a period of time. However, bodies of work like this may be better presented as ePortfolios, which are a popular way for learners to demonstrate their achievements and competencies, particularly in apprenticeships.

Collecting work-based evidence

Work-based learning is a topic on its own; however, an important issue when embedding eAssessment in the workplace is choosing appropriate digital technology that minimises learner interruption to their work. Work-based learning is naturally focused on 'real work' and acquiring industry knowledge, skills and experience, so assessment and feedback should be wrapped around this concept rather than being an intrusive addition. A digital experience for apprenticeships is achievable; however, you should aim to use a wide range of blended and flipped approaches.

When designing for work-based learning, it is highly important to identify on-, off- and near-the-job learning first, then decide on the most suitable digital technology to facilitate each process. Holistic assessment is advantageous here as it allows learners to demonstrate different criteria and units at the same time. Designing holistic assessment for work-based learning is time-consuming but is very effective once set up. You can add a digital layer to it by using links to the VLE for resources and activities for learners to complete as well as independently submitting evidence. This allows for a wide range of holistic evidence demonstrating both cognitive- and skills-based competencies. It also makes the process a more learner-centred approach and self-directed, allowing you more time to focus on other assessment activities. Visit the links at the end of this chapter for further guidance.

ePortfolios

An ePortfolio is a digital tool or system that enables learners to collect and organise multi-media artefacts such as text, hyperlinks, images, video and audio to present their work and learning experiences. An ePortfolio becomes a product of learning and achievement which learners can build upon throughout their learning journey. ePortfolios support an array of learning approaches such as reflection, self-directed learning and assessment of and for learning. The main benefits of ePortfolios are that they encourage reflective learning, support personal development, and increase the self-awareness and esteem of learners. This is because the ePortfolio is the product of the learner by ownership by demonstrating their individuality, abilities, aspirations and ambitions, containing learning, knowledge, experiences and achievements. Additionally, an ePortfolio can act as a transferable dem-onstration of achievement if a learner moves to another institution, progresses into higher education or employment. As well as the advantages of digital technology previously men-tioned, the following are significant benefits of using ePortfolios:

» Excellent for encouraging reflection and evaluating own work.

» Supports lifelong learning; the ability to use it before, during and after the programme.

» Can represent different starting points on a learner journey/achievement.

If ePortfolios can be effectively designed and integrated at the centre of a learner's assessment, it will enable the learner to be more independent and in control of their learning and development. Figure 4.1 illustrates a typical flow of a learner working with an ePortfolio, a process which they can enter at any point. Access a range of available ePortfolio tools from C4LPT (http://c4lpt.co.uk/directory-of-learning-performance-tools/notetaking-pim).

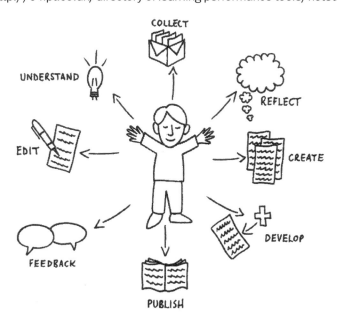

Figure 4.1. Illustrating how an ePortfolio is constructed.

ILT in quality assurance

With the right choice of digital technologies, you can use them to improve quality assurance systems and processes. Table 4.2 describes some ways of using digital technology in your quality assurance practices.

Table 4.2. Describing some ways to use digital technology in quality assurance practices.

Digital technology	Sampling	Standardisation
ePortfolios	You could ask assessors to send you hyperlinks to the ePortfolios which have been selected for sampling. Plus you are not carrying physical files with you. Most ePortfolios have the ability to allow you to leave assessor or internal verifier comments for others to see, but not by learners.	This will allow assessors to remotely check other assessor and internal verifiers' judgements and feedback wherever you have an internet connection. You could also create an exemplar ePortfolio for learners to aspire to and for assessors to know what to look for.
Online discussion	Microsoft Skype (www.skype. com) is a useful tool to keep all assessors and internal verifiers up to date as well as share samples of learners' work, whether they are on site or not. Each assessor could send you samples of work or use webcam live to show what is being done. It could also provide a really good question-and-answer function for assessors not on site.	All assessors could join a webinar and take part in a virtual standardisation meeting with a discussion and reviewing samples of work and practice.

Digital technology	Sampling	Standardisation
Online collaborative document	This would be an excellent way to distribute a sampling plan to all assessors and internal verifiers. Each team member could then update the document where necessary. It's instant and accessible by all. Each assessor could contribute to this collaborative sampling plan. It will give a sense of ownership and keep everyone on track. It could be colour coded by each assessor and unit.	Microsoft Teams (access via Office 365) is ideal to manage quality assurance processes as it captures all communication and document production in dedicated 'channels'. The team could identify good practice in learners work and markup so that assessors and internal verifiers can to refer to it.
Online wall/ pinboard	A visual tool like Padlet (https:// padlet.com) can be used to display all samples and learners' work. Feedback can be left under each piece of work and used for developmental initiatives. You could sample pieces of work from this and give feedback and support using web links where necessary.	This could visually bring together all assessors, samples and learners' work in one area. It can then be easily shared with the team as a collection and developmental resource.
Video/audio	Recording equipment such as digital cameras and voice recorders can be generally used to record learner skills and conversations. They provide reliable evidence to show performance and knowledge. The video/audio outputs can provide real hands-on evidence that gives a more rounded vision of what work is being done.	The video/audio outputs can be used to discuss in greater depth what learners are producing and how their work compares to others'. Moreover, recording their own assessor practice such as carrying out observations, conducting professional discussions with learners or even screencast tutorials of completing documents can be extremely useful. These could then be shared with the team to discuss strengths and limitations.

Digital technology	Sampling	Standardisation
VLE	Assessors could upload work or gather work in a programme area on the VLE. You could take the samples of work that have been uploaded via the assignment feature and also give feedback to assessors using this method.	While a VLE is not a document management system, the team could use an area of the VLE to clearly see all tracking and progression of all sampling submitted. It can be a really good audit mechanism.

Practical Task

» Reflect on your quality assurance practices and identify areas where you can utilise digital technology further to improve your processes.

Summary

This chapter explained the benefits of eAssessment approaches and a range of digital methods you can use to record, check, test and assess learning. It also explored how digital technologies can be used to enhance your quality assurance tasks and activities.

References and further reading

Armitage, A and Cogger, A (2019, forthcoming) *The New Apprenticeships: Facilitating Learning, Mentoring, Coaching and Assessing*. Northwich: Critical Publishing Ltd.

Gravells, A (2015) *Principles and Practices of Assessment: A Guide for Assessors in the FE and Skills Sector*. London: Learning Matters.

Gravells, A (2016) *Principles and Practices of Quality Assurance: A Guide for Internal and External Quality Assurers in the FE and Skills Sector*. London: Learning Matters.

Jisc (2007) *Effective Practice with e-Assessment*. London: HEFCE.

Jisc (2008) *Effective Practice with e-Portfolios*. London: HEFCE.

Read, H and Gravells, A (2015) *The Best Vocational Trainer's Guide: Essential Knowledge and Skills for Those Responsible for Workplace Learning*. Bideford: Read On Publications.

Read, H (2012) *The Best Quality Assurer's Guide: For IQAs and EQAs of Vocational Qualifications*. Bideford. Read On Publications.

Read, H (2013) *The Best Initial Assessment Guide: Getting it Right – from the Start*. Bideford: Read On Publications.

Read, H (2016) *The Best Assessor's Guide: Essential Knowledge and Skills for Vocational Assessors* (2nd edition). Bideford: Read On Publications.

Scott, D (2015, 5 December) *A View of Interaction*. [online] Available at: http://danielscott86.blogspot.com/2015/12/a-view-of-interaction.html (accessed 11 June 2018).

Scott, D (2016, 11 February) *Designing for Project Based Learning*. [online] Available at: http://danielscott86.blogspot.com/2016/02/designing-for-project-based-learning.html (accessed 11 June 2018).

Scott, D (2018, 15 June) *Digital apprenticeships – a brief Q&A*. [online] Available at: http://danielscott86.blogspot.com/2018/06/digital-apprenticeships-a-brief-qa.html (accessed 15 June 2018).

Useful websites

» C4LPT – Quizzing & testing tools – http://c4lpt.co.uk/directory-of-learning-performance-tools/quizzing-testing-tools
» Jisc – Transforming assessment and feedback with technology – www.jisc.ac.uk/guides/transforming-assessment-and-feedback
» Jisc – Making a difference to assessment and feedback – www.jisc.ac.uk/reports/the-evolution-of-feltag#assess

» Jisc – Guides – Assessment – https://tinyurl.com/yag3yc94

» Jisc – Digital apprenticeships – www.jisc.ac.uk/rd/projects/digital-apprenticeships

» PebblePad – Publications, Conferences and Events – https://community.pebblepad. co.uk/support/solutions/folders/13000005993

Chapter 5 Evaluate

Chapter content

This chapter covers the following topics:

» evaluating your own use of ILT;

» introducing learning analytics, including the use of learner data.

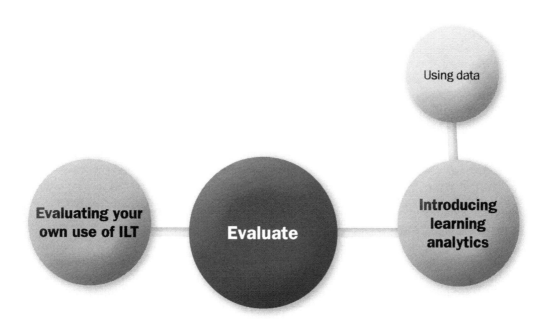

Introduction

In the previous chapters, you have read how using ILT in your practices brings many benefits for you and your learners. However, how aware are you of the impact that ILT has on you and your learners? Apart from observing learners in the classroom using devices or confirming they've been online in a VLE, how do you know the impact ILT has on them? As for yourself, how has ILT enhanced or transformed your practices? This chapter invites you to evaluate your use of ILT and the ILT choices you made that have a positive impact on your practices and your learners' learning.

Evaluating your own use of ILT

At the end of your taught sessions you may already obtain feedback from your students on how the session went, along with the impact of what they have learned. This might include the resources you used and activities using ILT.

Determining the impact of the ranges of ILT you have used can be a challenging task, because you cannot put a number on it. You can however give it a direction by using something akin to a Likert scale. But it is very important that you and your learners know what they have gained from the experience. As discussed in Chapter 1, ILT can sometimes be misused in that it can 'dazzle' your learners but have no underpinning pedagogical rationale. Therefore, it is important to assess how successful and effective the ILT was that you used. This requires you to reflect on your learning design, instructional methods and support you provided to your learners. Ultimately, anything that improves the experience and quality of learning and its outcomes achieved through digital technology is likely to be positive. It may help to put yourself in a learner's position to understand the purpose and effect of the activities you choose and design with digital technology.

Evaluating your use of ILT is an important task as it allows you to:

» know how appropriate your choice of ILT was to support learning engagement, inter-action and teaching delivery;

» consider how effective the online resources and activities are in supporting your learners and programme requirements;

» identify opportunities to improve and enhance your practices.

Reflective Task

» Critically analyse how ILT supported and enhanced you in your role. Think about the impact ILT has on:

  • learner performance and experience;

  • organisational performance and development;

  • your subject areas;

  • the identity and performance of your own role.

» Use experiences and own reflections of your use of ILT with learners.

» Think of the learning approaches, methods and activities you used. Did they help learners to manage their learning better and help make choices for what comes next?

» Collect feedback from your learners on how they learned with ILT and whether they perceive that it enhanced their learning experience.

Practical Task

If you have an online space for your learners (a VLE) or have created an online activity or resource, you may want to evaluate the following areas or gain feedback from learners. However, note that not all learning opportunities aspire to cover all these points in every situation.

» How well can you navigate and orientate yourself around the VLE and other areas of the online activity?

» Overall, is the VLE layout clear and well-structured in explaining what you are expected to do?

» Is there a wide variety and types of online activities and resources available in the VLE?

> » Are the online activities and resources in the VLE signposted well so you can get what you want easily?

> » Do the online activities and resources have clear instructions on their purpose, sequence and schedule (time/length)?

> » Do the choices of online activities and resources in the VLE add value to the learning and support you in achieving the learning requirements?

> » Do the interactive learning objects support you well in understanding the learning requirements?

> » Is there an adequate range of online activities to support and allow you to socialise and share ideas and experiences with peers and tutors?

> » Are the online activities and resources useful in preparing you for my programme assessments?

> » Is there an adequate range of features/options to ask for support on learning, technical and administrative issues?

> » Do you use any other online tools and resources to support your learning, if so what are they?

> » Can you suggest any improvements to the way that I deliver online learning to you? For example, do you have any specific needs that ought to be addressed?

Introducing learning analytics

ILT has an added bonus of providing opportunities to collect data on individuals or groups that can be used in various ways to improve the learner experience, programme and organisation. Usually this data is used to analyse learner progress for grading. It is part of eLearning but more related to the administration of it. Every time a learner logs into a VLE, online service or tool and interacts with activities, resources and their peers online, they leave data, often called learning analytics. This may also be referred to as data analytics, which enables you to collect, analyse and report large datasets to identify the patterns and trends of your learners. Therefore, this data can be used to inform learner activity, behaviour and preferences around how they learn and interact with digital content. Learning analytics should not only be used to capture what your learners have done or are doing, but they have scope to inform and improve future online learning design, online learning interactions, assessment needs and digital marketing of online courses and provisions. Perhaps you could encourage your learners to manage their own learning, for example using progress trackers in a VLE so that they can monitor their own performance and achievement on online activities.

Using your own and your learners' experiences, extract the key points and try to turn them into positive developments for future lessons. This changes insight to foresight and enables you to be better informed about what you could adapt and improve in your practices. However, try not to get too hung up on the data you collect. While data can be interesting, the tools can also be distracting. Focus on how you can leverage the data to improve processes and outcomes and listen to your own in-built teacher instincts. Be mindful of any trends that appear. However, it's not just about following trends but setting and progressing them for the future. Trends change instantly while results are permanent. Think about how the data can be used to inspire innovation.

Your employer may have a VLE or tutorial and grading system in place that generates reports of the data you want. These may be located within the system or on some kind of dashboard for you to access. Work with your learning technologists or colleagues to help you interpret the data and to identify appropriate interventions utilising it.

Practical Task

If you don't have a VLE and/or reporting system to collect data, try Google Analytics (https://analytics.google.com) or Google Data Studio (https://datastudio.google.com). These tools can be used to gather data to determine when learners are most active on your VLE or on another site you may have. You can also find out when, how and where they are accessing digital activities and resources, which can be useful for induction and training purposes. This data might be helpful when producing reports for quality review meetings on user engagement. You may be able to determine how long and how active your learners are on your VLE or online materials and you might find that your learner's login time has increased. This might be a sign that learners are spending longer in their VLE programme space, which could mean the quality of your online learning material has improved.

Using data

If you are going to evaluate and use learner data in various ways internally and externally to your organisation, it is good practice to seek permission from your learners first. It is important that learners need to know what data is being collected, why you are wanting to use it, who has access to their data and how they can access it. The data you collect should be used for a specified purpose, such as informing your learning, teaching and assessment practices.

In terms of collecting and using learner data, your organisation will have policies and procedures you must comply with, such as the General Data Protection Regulation (GDPR) in the United Kingdom. GDPR replaced the Data Protection Act (1998) and was introduced in May 2018 in response to the advances in digital technology and the large volumes of electronic data stored. The legislation requires you to only access and process data that is relevant to the job you do, and that you only share data with people who are legitimately entitled to have access to it. Access the links at the end of this chapter to learn more about GDPR and how it applies to you.

Summary

This chapter covered the importance of evaluating your use of ILT and reflecting on certain aspects of your ILT practices. You were introduced to learning analytics and how the data can be used to inform future ILT practices as well as overall learner performance. The use of learner data was explained, together with how you might need approval before commencing collecting data.

References and further reading

Harasim, L (2017) *Learning Theory and Online Technologies*. London: Routledge.

Ingle, S and Duckworth, V (2013) *Enhancing Learning Through Technology in Lifelong Learning: Fresh Ideas: Innovative Strategies*. Maidenhead: Open University Press.

Jisc (nd) *Code of Practice for Learning Analytics*. [online] Available at: www.jisc.ac.uk/guides/code-of-practice-for-learning-analytics (accessed 11 June 2018).

Luckin, R (2018) *Enhancing Learning and Teaching with Technology: What the Research Says*. London: UCL IOE Press.

Scott, D (2014, 6 May) *Observing ILT*. [online] Available at: http://danielscott86.blogspot.com/2014/05/observing-ilt.html (accessed 11 June 2018).

Scott, D (2017, 2 May) *Evaluating Technology Enhanced Learning*. [online] Available at: http://danielscott86.blogspot.com/2017/05/evaluating-technology-enhanced-learning.html (accessed 11 June 2018).

Sharrock, T (2019) *Using Lesson Observation to Improve Learning: Practical Strategies for FE and Post-16 Tutors*. Northwich: Critical Publishing Ltd.

Useful websites

» Gov.uk – Data protection: toolkit for schools (including compliance with GDPR – may also help training organisations and colleges) – https://tinyurl.com/y8feyy5n

» Jisc – General Data Protection Regulation (GDPR) – www.jisc.ac.uk/gdpr

» University of York – York TEL Handbook – https://elearningyork.wordpress.com/learning-design-and-development/technology-enhanced-learning-handbook/york-tel-handbook-7-evaluation-and-development

Chapter 6 Keep up to date

Chapter content

This chapter covers the following topics:

» continuing professional development, including CPD opportunities;

» conferences and events, including CMALT;

» social media and social networking, including peer collaboration;

» promoting your ILT practices.

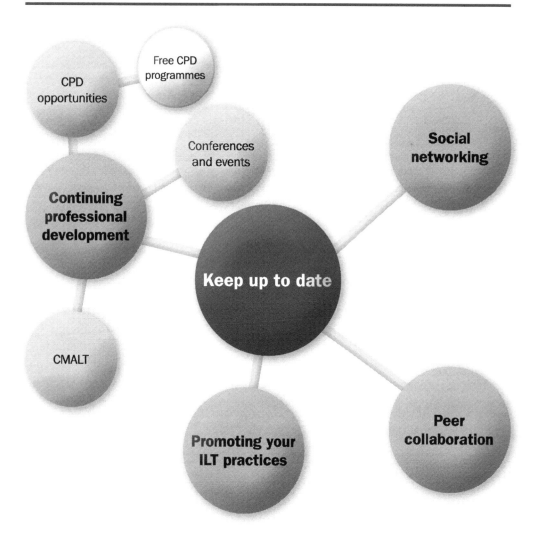

Introduction

As an educator it is important to keep up to date with your subject-specialist expertise and emerging teaching practices. This is a process known as continuing professional development (CPD): retaining, maintaining and developing your professional credibility with your learners and organisation. While it can be challenging to find suitable and appropriate training and the time to participate, it is essential for your professional growth and to ensure that your learners are taught up-to-date knowledge, skills and relevant legislation. CPD is also important in learning about new tools and resources that can enhance your practices. However, it's not just about knowing the latest thing, but about designing great teaching and learning though technology. It's good to be on top of your game, to keep abreast of changes and emerging and trending digital technologies.

This final chapter summarises how you can keep up to date with the growing abundance of digital technologies and their potential contribution to learning. It introduces you to some ways that you can get up to speed on the latest ILT trends, engage and collaborate with other professionals, promote your own good practice and join courses or professional bodies/associations.

Continuing professional development

CPD is not just about staying current in your specialist subject, but includes face-to-face, blended and online pedagogies and organisational and national policies. All of these will positively impact on your job role and improve and enhance your practices. Another reason to embrace CPD is to stay current and validated, especially in the use of ILT, as those who use ILT most effectively are agile when meeting the demands and challenges of twenty-first-century learning.

To effectively plan and facilitate your CPD, it's useful to have an action plan of the things you wish to experiment with, develop, implement and evaluate to enhance your practices. At the same time, keep an eye open (or have others do it for you) for new ideas in designing teaching and assessment. Having a plan makes it more likely that you will investigate and apply what you set out to do and reflect on its success. It's important to not become complacent in your knowledge, skills and experience – be proactive and take the lead on your own development. The more effort and involvement you put into your professional development, the richer your knowledge, skills and experience will become.

Below is a list of organisations and bodies that offer professional support and are relevant to the further education and skills sectors.

» Association for Research in Post-Compulsory Education (ARPCE) – http://arpce.org.uk

» Association of Colleges (AoC) – www.aoc.co.uk

» Association of Employment and Learning Providers (AELP) – www.aelp.org.uk

» Chartered Institute for Educational Assessors – www.herts.ac.uk/ciea/chartered-institute-of-educational-assessors

» Chartered Institute of Personnel and Development (CIPD) – www.cipd.co.uk

» The Chartered Institution for Further Education – www.fecharter.org.uk

» Chartered Management Institute – www.managers.org.uk

» Education and Training Foundation (ETF) – www.et-foundation.co.uk

» Electronic Platform for Adult Learning in Europe (EPALE) – https://ec.europa.eu/epale

» FE News – www.fenews.co.uk

» FE Week – https://feweek.co.uk

» General Teaching Council for Northern Ireland (GTCNI) – www.gtcni.org.uk

» HOLEX – http://holex.org.uk

» The Institute of Training and Occupational Learning (ITOL) – www.itol.org

» International Professional Development Association (IPDA) – http://ipda.org.uk

» Learning and Skills Research Network – https://lsrn.wordpress.com

» Learning and Work Institute – www.learningandwork.org.uk

» National Education Union – https://neu.org.uk

» Society for Education and Training (SET) – https://set.et-foundation.co.uk

» Tutor Voices – https://tutorvoicesblog.wordpress.com

» University and College Union (UCU) – www.ucu.org.uk

» Workers' Educational Association (WEA) – www.wea.org.uk

Reflective Task

» Using Appendix 6.1 (and considering Appendix 1.1), reflect on your current practices and the contents of the previous chapters. Identify and list areas you wish to explore further or implement in your practices. For example, what new digital tools and resources do you want to try out? How do you want to digitally enhance your curriculum offering? Perhaps you want to identify people to collaborate with or observe others' use of ILT? You might like to take this time to think about:

  • What digital capabilities would you like to develop?

  • What barriers may affect you in developing your digital capabilities?

» As well as preparing a Personal and Professional Development Plan, you may want to include digital capabilities in your own appraisal process to track progress and development.

» Use Appendix 6.2 to log your progress and evaluation, and update it frequently.

CPD opportunities

Higher education courses are good opportunities to learn about underpinning theories and pedagogies, build new professional relationships with like-minded others, and learn about new kinds of ILT and how to use them in the classroom. Several universities offer distance, blended, taught or research-based ILT programmes at both undergraduate and postgraduate levels. If this interests you, do research locally and nationally to see what different institutions have to offer and the potential costs. Alternatively, you may be interested in the following vocational qualifications that may be offered locally:

» Level 1 Award in Digital Technologies for Learning

» Level 3 Award and Diploma in Digital Learning Design

» Level 4 Diploma and Extended Diploma in Digital Learning Design

» Level 4 Award in Digital Learning for Educators

» Level 4 Award for Technology Enabled Educators

» Level 4 Certificate in Technology in Learning Delivery

Free CPD programmes

Many organisations and universities offer free online courses, called MOOCs (Massive Open Online Courses), which are often short or 'taster' courses. MOOCs are delivered online or in a VLE and are usually open internationally, meaning that the courses typically have a large cohort, giving you the opportunity to connect with like-minded individuals from around the world. You are expected to be self-motivated and navigate yourself through the course; however, there are online tutors to help. The more aspects of a MOOC you participate and collaborate in, the more you will gain from it.

Most MOOCs are free; however, some charge for obtaining a certificate of completion and course materials. Below is a range of free online courses that you can join and participate in.

» Alison – https://alison.com

» Coursera – www.coursera.org

» edX – www.edx.org

» FutureLearn – Blended Learning Essentials: Getting Started – www.futurelearn.com/courses/blended-learning-getting-started

» FutureLearn – Blended Learning Essentials: Embedding Practice – www.futurelearn.com/courses/blended-learning-embedding-practice

» FutureLearn – Blended Learning Essentials: Developing Digital Skills – www.futurelearn.com/courses/blended-learning-digital-skills

» FutureLearn – Blended Learning Essentials: Digitally-Enriched Apprenticeships – www.futurelearn.com/courses/blended-learning-digitally-enriched-apprenticeships

- » Google for Education: Training Center – https://edutrainingcenter.withgoogle.com
- » Khan Academy – www.khanacademy.org
- » Lynda.com – www.lynda.com
- » The Open University OpenLearn – www.open.edu/openlearn/free-courses
- » Udemy – www.udemy.com

A comprehensive list of MOOCs from universities, colleges and other educators can be found here at (www.mooc-list.com). Just enter the details of a course you are looking for, search, and then review the course opportunities presented.

Remember when researching any course to look carefully at what is being taught and who is presenting the learning, and consider how participation will benefit you and impact on your role. Some ILT courses may focus on the technology aspect when you need the pedagogy to be the main focus. You may still want to do this as general CPD, and your employer may take an interest in what you are doing as it benefits other practitioners.

Conferences and events

The following conferences and events are very popular for learning about new ILT and eLearning practice. They are also a good opportunity for networking with other educators.

- » ALT – www.alt.ac.uk/events
- » ALT Annual Conference – www.alt.ac.uk/altc
- » Bett Show – www.bettshow.com
- » CIPD Learning and Development Show – www2.cipd.co.uk/events/learning-development-show
- » FE News – www.fenews.co.uk/events
- » Jisc – www.jisc.ac.uk/events
- » Learning Technologies – www.learningtechnologies.co.uk
- » UKFEchat – www.ukfechat.com

CMALT

The Certified Membership of the Association for Learning Technology (CMALT) (www.alt.ac.uk/certified-membership) is a peer-assessed professional accreditation scheme. Preparing a CMALT submission allows you to demonstrate and certify your practices, experience and capabilities in effective use of ILT. It enables you to follow a supportive pathway for developing your ILT practices that is aligned to your own context alongside other aspirational educators. Many CMALT holders are ILT practitioners, teachers and researchers from across the educational and commercial sectors.

Employers are increasingly including CMALT as a 'desirable' criterion on their job specifications when recruiting for teaching and ILT-related roles. So CMALT can be invaluable in getting your practices professionally accredited and has the added bonus of enabling you to become part of a supportive and collaborative community.

Social networking

Because the internet has become a highly accessible resource for information and making connections to people, it increases our opportunities to seek out more knowledge but to ensure it is accurate and up to date. Acquiring information and developing ideas from others digitally has become so much easier with the abundance of social media technologies, as Figure 6.1 overleaf illustrates. Social media tools are an easy way of keeping up to date with what's happening in the ILT field. The use of hashtags has made navigating social media a lot easier. Hashtags are simply a way of 'tagging' something to be easily found by others. Most people use key words associated with what they have shared. On most if not all social media platforms you have the ability to select hashtags that will bring up all shared content with that tag. On Twitter for example, you will see key words hyperlinked with the # character. You can search on various topics or people to find learning and teaching ideas, resources and potential people with whom you might collaborate. To find influential people and organisations to follow, search on the internet for 'Jisc Top 10 Further Education Social Media Superstars' or 'Tes Edtech 50' – a list of those who have been shaping ILT in the sector.

Social media can still be used even if you don't feel ready to post anything yourself. This is termed 'positive silent engagement'. You could start off gently by following a few people or discussion threads and then set yourself a challenge to post your thoughts once you feel comfortable to do so. Once you start receiving 'likes' or comments back from fellow educators or students, it will encourage wider sharing going forward.

Some educators now hold live discussions on Twitter under relevant hashtags. Examples include the UKFEchat (https://twitter.com/theukfechat) or the Learning and Teaching in HE Tweetchat (https://twitter.com/LTHEchat). Questions are posted by the organisers and people respond with answers including the hashtag – a good way to crowdsource knowledge and ideas. A popular Twitter account is TeacherToolkit (https://twitter.com/TeacherToolkit), which has various resources and a large collaborative network. Why not share your learning, ideas and thoughts about this book using the hashtag, #LTbookFE?

Assessors and internal and external verifiers may want to join this LinkedIn group 'RQF/QCF/NVQ Assessors, IQAs and EQAs' (www.linkedin.com/groups/2668109). However, do search for other teaching groups to join.

Figure 6.1. Illustrating where knowledge resides in digital technology and within people.

Practical Task

» Using Twitter, LinkedIn, Facebook (www.facebook.com) or any other social media platform, search on those sites with key words of interest to you. The search results will bring up individuals or groups that you could connect with and join.

» Click on any that interest you and review the content that the individual or group is presenting. Is the information useful? How much will you gain from them – are they sharing websites, ideas or viewpoints? How often do they share this information?

Ideally, define a list of enthusiastic and passionate people and organisations that you can refer to on a regular basis for instant know-how. You may want to ask yourself why you should explore and devote time to learning something new. What examples are there that you can relate to and generally use? Can you find material for further reading that is understandable for non-experts?

Once you have completed the activity above, you can manage the settings on your account to receive updates daily, weekly or monthly. The update emails generate 'highlights/updates in your network' of the content shared by the users you follow. This then allows you to sift through content that you are interested in. So it is important to follow people that share meaningful content rather than just personal updates.

Practical Task

» Try creating your own personal learning network (PLN) that pulls in all the content that you want. For example, people or organisations sharing resources, ideas, networking groups and conferences; connect/follow credible educators and researchers; ask questions or for help on things you need support with.

» This could involve creating social bookmarks: another form of tagging that allows you to annotate and organise web pages. Try (https://del.icio.us) or (www.diigo.com) to bookmark websites or personal blogs that frequently post out useful content. Or you could use a feature in Twitter called Lists that allows you to add people or organisations to a list you have created, such as specific topics or industries. You can then adjust your settings so you can receive news updates and top stories daily, weekly or monthly.

» Some Twitter accounts follow educational bloggers and compile them into lists like edublogs (https://twitter.com/edublogs).

» Why not consider making your PLN open access so that others can view it and perhaps contribute?

News aggregators like Pocket (https://getpocket.com) are useful as you can cherry-pick social media content and put it aside to read later. RSS (Really Simple Syndication) feeds are a good way to aggregate news content. RSS is a web-based feed providing a summary of the latest updates from a website. They're useful to keep you up to date without actually visiting numerous websites. Check a website's news section to see if you can subscribe to that news feed or copy the RSS feed and place it into sites like Feedly (https://feedly.com). Sign up to websites such as eLearning Feeds and eLearning Industry to keep up to date with current ILT practices and eLearning designs. YouTube (www.youtube.com) is an excellent source for finding talks, screencasts containing examples of good practice and playlists. TED Talks (www.ted.com) are a great way of keeping up to date with new and critical thinking. TeachThought (www.teachthought.com), Edutopia (www.edutopia.org), Edudemic (www.edudemic.com) and Hybrid Pedagogy (http://hybridpedagogy.org) are useful websites to acquire new perspectives and ideas.

Peer collaboration

A helpful way to see how ILT is used in context with your subject is to observe others. In your organisation you may be able to participate in team peer observations, where colleagues can sit in on lessons and observe the whole session or just certain aspects. This allows you to see what digital technology your colleagues are using and how they are using it. It's a good idea to investigate opportunities both internal and external to your organisation to see if there are any collaborative meetings or informal events like TeachMeets in which you can gain insights or participate in. You could even ask any colleagues to see if they are open to being observed using ILT. If you have advanced practitioners in your organisation, why not speak to one of them to see how you can become involved? You may even want to think about setting up your own collaborative group so you can share good practices with each other.

Practical Task

» Try to set up a peer observation. Make a list of ILT practices you want to see in action and ask others if you can observe them. Make sure you take a pen and some paper to make notes.

» You can then modify your own session plans to incorporate and try those new ideas. Remember to keep a note of what worked well.

Promoting your ILT practices

When networking with others it's not all about taking from others, but about giving back to individuals, groups, and the sector as a whole. It helps to promote the benefits of ILT and enable its wider use in the sector. Take the opportunity to showcase your good practice or to get feedback on something you are developing or intending to do. If you feel confident about your practices, you may want to help others who are less confident by sharing your experience and ideas with them. Below are some ways you can promote your ILT practices.

» Deliver a small-scale session (a micro-teach) to your peers, and include:

- how you used ILT and the impact it had on you and your learners;

- your experience of using ILT on others and detail the features, benefits and limitations of it;

- lesson evaluations of your learners' experiences and any useful resources and links for others to follow up and use.

» Present at conferences and events.

» Record a video or audio of you demonstrating or discussing the ILT you have tried.

» Design and share an online resource or activity.

» Post a short description of recent or past practices.

» Write a blog post or case study of an aspect of your practice or review ILT you have used.

» Share your blog post or review and use it as a vehicle for others to access the good practice you have generated.

You may feel inspired to reflect upon your efforts and practices through a blog, ePortfolio or website. You could promote this alongside your professional social media and encourage others to comment as a way to gain feedback and promote collaboration.

> ### Example
>
> *Ann is an FE teacher in a large London college. She reflects regularly on her practice and experiences by writing a blog post. She posts an update at least once a week discussing the use of ILT in her lessons and how effective it was. She then shares this on her Twitter account using relevant hashtags so that others can find it when searching. She also enables comments on her posts to encourage contributions from others.*

Summary

This chapter has introduced you to some of the ways in which you can keep up to date in the field of ILT, both in your workplace and online. Using these approaches and accessing the websites mentioned in this chapter will help you to keep up to date and empower your professional relationships with others inside and outside your organisation, ultimately enhancing your learner's learning.

References and further reading

Appleyard, K and Appleyard, N (2015) *Reflective Teaching and Learning in Further Education*. Northwich: Critical Publishing Ltd.

Armitage, A, Evershed, J, Hayes, D, Hudson, A, Kent, J, Lawes, S, Poma, S and Renwick, M (2012) *Teaching and Training in Lifelong Learning* (4th edition). Maidenhead: Open University Press, McGraw-Hill Education.

Gibbs, G (1988) *Learning by Doing: A Guide to Teaching and Learning Methods*. Oxford: Further Education Unit, Oxford Polytechnic.

Lambe, J and Morris, N (2014) *Palgrave Study Skills: Studying a MOOC*. Palgrave Macmillan.

Machin, L, Hindmarch, D, Murray, S and Richardson, T (2016) Information and Communication Technology for Learning, in *A Complete Guide to the Level 5 Diploma in Education and Training* (2nd edition). Northwich. Critical Publishing Ltd.

Petty, G (2014) *Teaching Today: A Practical Guide* (5th edition). Oxford: Oxford University Press.

Scott, D (2018, 10 July) ALT – An Imprinting Celebration. [online] Available at: http://danielscott86.blogspot.com/2018/07/alt-imprinting-celebration.html (accessed 11 July 2018).

Siemens, G (2004) *Connectivism: A Learning Theory for the Digital Age*. Elearnspace.

Useful websites

» #1minuteCPD – https://1minutecpd.wordpress.com
» ALT Research in Learning Technology (RLT) – https://journal.alt.ac.uk/index.php/rlt
» Ann Gravells Ltd – www.anngravells.com
» Association for Learning Technology – www.alt.ac.uk
» EDUCAUSE – www.educause.edu
» eLearning Feeds – http://elearningfeeds.com
» eLearning Industry – https://elearningindustry.com
» Education and Training Foundation (ETF) – Digital Skills Support – www.et-foundation.co.uk/supporting/support-practitioners/digital-skills-support
» Excellence Gateway – www.excellencegateway.org.uk
» Future Teacher Talks – https://xot.futureteacher.eu/play.php?template_id=4
» Jisc – www.jisc.ac.uk
» Microsoft Education – www.microsoft.com/education
» Read On Publications Ltd – https://readonpublications.co.uk
» Teacher Training Videos – www.teachertrainingvideos.com
» UCISA – www.ucisa.ac.uk/events

Glossary

There are countless digital technologies and names associated with ILT and eLearning. The following is a glossary that covers some of the ones you are most likely to come across in your role.

Term	Description
Augmented reality (AR)	Adding a digital layer over real-world environments and situations.
Blended learning	Using both face-to-face and ICT for delivering learning.
Blog	Web log, a kind of online diary to publish multimedia content.
Clickbait	Content on the internet purposely designed to attract attention that encourages you to select on a link that takes you to a web page.
Cloud-based platforms/storage	A network of remote servers hosted on the internet to provide services rather than a local server on your personal computer.
Digital technology	In the context of education: electronic devices, websites and online media that can enhance assistive and social learning and teaching tasks.
Distance learning	Delivering learning and teaching remotely – often online.
eBook	A digital book that can be read on desktop and mobile devices.
eLearning	Pedagogy that can be used within learning technology.
eLearning object	Referred to as an interactive online activity containing multimedia content.
ePortfolio	An electronic portfolio containing a body of digital evidence in the form of multimedia content.
Face-to-face teaching	A traditional method of delivering teaching and learning that is distinguishable from an online environment.
Firewall	Protection against unauthorised access to a personal computer or network.

Learning technology	Tools and systems that can support and manage learning.
Mobile learning	Use of mobile devices to facilitate learning and teaching.
Multimedia	Text, images, audio, video and animation combined.
Open badges	A digital badge that demonstrates an accomplishment, knowledge or skill; typically in a VLE.
Pedagogy	Methods, strategies and styles of facilitating learning and teaching.
Personal Learning Network (PLN)	Utilising and combining personal and organisational digital technologies and content.
Podcast	A downloadable audio file.
QR code	Quick Response barcode that stores URLs and other information readable by a camera, typically on a mobile device.
Really Simple Syndication (RSS)	A method to pull and push content online.
Screencast	Software that can capture movements on your screen.
Self-paced learning	Typically in an asynchronous environment, where the individual controls the pace of their learning.
Troll	Someone that deliberately posts provocative content online to cause arguments.
Virtual learning environment (VLE)	An online space that allows you to create and manage digital learning and teaching activities and resources.
Webinar	A seminar that is delivered online. Also used for online tutorials and workshops.
Wi-Fi	A facility that allows devices to be connected to the internet.
Wiki	A series of web pages that can be openly edited.

Appendix 1.1

Teacher questions (FE and skills) – adapted from the Jisc Digital Discovery Tool pilot project (2018)

The Jisc Digital Discovery Tool aims to broadly explore and encourage reflection on your personal digital capability strengths and weaknesses. It provides personal reports that contain relevant and useful resources to support your development. Access this link (www.jisc.ac.uk/rd/projects/building-digital-capability) to learn more about the tool.

The following questions have been taken from the specialist assessment 'digital teaching', which focuses on capabilities for staff working in the further education and skills sector. There are three types of questions for each of the eight headings that make up this assessment:

1. **Confidence questions** – rate your confidence with a digital practice or skill.

2. **Depth questions** – select the one response out of four that best describes your approach to a digital task.

3. **Breadth questions** – select all the digital activities that you do, from a range of six.

Use the outcomes of this to understand more about your own digital capabilities and to determine areas of support that you may need.

Planning and preparation						
Confidence question Rate how confident you are designing digital activities to support different learning outcomes						
Confident	1	2	3	4	5	**Not confident**
Depth question Which best describes how you plan a learning session to include the use of digital technologies? ☐ I put in place any support I might need ☐ I plan around the digital technologies that are familiar to me ☐ I design digital activities to support the learning outcomes ☐ I have a range of digital activities I can deploy to meet learners' needs						

Breadth question

When planning a learning session or course, which of these do you do?

☐ Look for relevant examples or materials online

☐ Consider how students could use their own digital devices

☐ Check students have the digital skills they need

☐ Provide alternatives in case of any technical issues

☐ Try new digital technologies or approaches to challenge yourself

☐ Share your ideas online with other teaching professionals

Learning resources

Confidence question

Rate how confident you are about using digital resources within the rules of copyright

Confident	1	2	3	4	5	Not confident

Depth question

Which best describes your approach to choosing and using digital resources for learning?

☐ I provide digital learning resources when I have to

☐ I find quality learning resources to suit the topic I am teaching

☐ I find and adapt learning resources to meet my students' needs

☐ I create my own learning resources, drawing on the best example

Breadth question

Which of these resource types have you produced for your learners to use?

☐ Online quiz

☐ Video clip

☐ Voice-over slides

☐ Image or animation

☐ Web page or eLearning object

☐ Simulation, app or game

Accessibility and diversity

Confidence question

Rate how confident you are assessing digital tools or resources for their accessibility

Confident	1	2	3	4	5	Not confident

Depth question

How do you ensure students can access the digital learning opportunities you offer?

☐ I assume they have the devices and skills they need

☐ I signpost students to sources of support

☐ I check they have the devices and skills they need for any new activity

☐ I design activities that let students showcase different digital skills

Breadth question

Which of these measures have you taken to support digital inclusion?

☐ Help learners to use assistive software or interfaces

☐ Use legible fonts and colour contrasts

☐ Provide text alternatives to visual media

☐ Check students have equitable access to devices

☐ Design content to be mobile-friendly

☐ Signpost students to sources of digital support

Face-to-face teaching

Confidence question

Rate how confident you are using presentation technologies in the classroom

Confident	1	2	3	4	5	Not confident

Depth question

Which best describes your approach to designing a digital presentation for students?

☐ I make sure I cover everything that's in the notes

☐ I choose images and layouts to make it visually engaging

☐ I use graphics, transitions and interactive elements such as polling

☐ I use educational design principles and a range of presentation media

Breadth question

Which of these digital activities take place in your face-to-face classes?

☐ Live polling/quizzing

☐ Live internet searches or missions

☐ Learners record ideas, eg via Padlet

☐ Learners make audio/video recordings

☐ Learners present their work in a digital medium

☐ Learners collaborate on digital projects

Online teaching						

Confidence question
Rate how confident you feel about teaching in a live online environment, eg webinar platform

Confident	1	2	3	4	5	Not confident

Depth question
Which of these best describes your approach to teaching online (whether you are working in a fully online or in a blended setting)?
☐ I try to leave online teaching to the specialists
☐ I am comfortable facilitating online discussions (text-based)
☐ I can teach in any online environment, eg webinar, text-based, video
☐ I use public media, eg Facebook, blogs, alongside an online platform

Breadth question
Which of these online activities do you set for your students?
☐ Live discussion (audio/chat)
☐ Forum discussion (not live)
☐ Collate links or references
☐ Collaborate on a presentation or project
☐ Review or annotate each other's work
☐ Contribute to a live wiki or blog

Supporting digital capabilities						

Confidence question
Rate how confident you are that you support students to become confident digital learners

Confident	1	2	3	4	5	Not confident

Depth question
Which best represents your attitude to the digital skills students need for work?
☐ Students discuss this with the careers/employability team
☐ I make sure students practise basic digital skills
☐ I set students digital tasks that reflect workplace trends
☐ I make digital futures a key theme for discussion and assessment

Breadth question

Which of these have you helped learners to achieve?

☐ Assess the credibility of online content

☐ Build a positive digital presence and identity

☐ Develop good digital study habits, eg note-making

☐ Digitally record and reflect on their learning

☐ Learn a new software application

☐ Model appropriate, responsible behaviour online

Assessment and feedback

Confidence question

Rate how confident you are about marking online assessments and recording student grades

Confident	1	2	3	4	5	Not confident

Depth question

Which best reflects your expertise in designing online tests?

☐ I can put traditional tests into an online environment

☐ I can write multiple choice questions and quizzes

☐ I use the full range of question types, eg labelling, ranking, grid

☐ I design engaging assessments using different learning media

Breadth question

Which of these can you do?

☐ Use data to monitor learners' progress

☐ Assess the quality of work in different digital media

☐ Set up and facilitate online peer review

☐ Support learners to collate and reflect on work in an ePortfolio

☐ Give feedback as digital audio or annotations

☐ Assess student performance using a simulation or game

Reflection and CPD

Confidence question

Rate how confident you are about keeping up with current practice in digital learning (ILT, eLearning, digital education)

Confident	1	2	3	4	5	Not confident

Depth question

Which best represents your approach to developing your digital practice as an educator?

☐ It is not a priority for me

☐ I learn to use the VLE and similar systems

☐ I look for opportunities to develop my digital practice further

☐ Digital education is central to my role and I enjoy sharing my expertise

Breadth question

Which of these have you done in the past year?

☐ Attend a live/online workshop on a digital topic

☐ Contribute to a live/online event on a digital topic

☐ Talk to a mentor / head of department about your digital skills

☐ Record your teaching practice (photo/video) for reflection

☐ Read an article about digital learning

☐ Share teaching materials online with other practitioners

Appendix 1.2

Digital capability curriculum mapping – adapted from Jisc (2017)

Based on Jisc's six elements of digital capabilities, use the table below to assess your curriculum or a smaller unit on how it prepares your learners in their own digital capabilities. Not every element may need to be used, but do consider including them in different ways.

Element	Curriculum considerations	How do learners do this in your programme or session (or how could they)?	How will learners gain practice and feedback on this?
ICT proficiency (functional skills)	Use **specialised digital tools** or practices of the subject area (eg design, data capture and analysis, monitoring, reporting, coding).		
	Use **generic digital tools** to achieve subject-related goals (eg devices, browsers, online services, productivity tools, media editors).		

Information, data and media literacies (critical use)	Find, evaluate and manage **digital information** relevant to the topics of study.		
	Find, analyse and use **digital data** in subject-specialist ways, and with attention to the ethics of data use.		
	Use **digital media** to learn and communicate ideas, and to present the outcomes of learning (eg videos, presentations, wikis).		
Digital creation, problem solving and innovation (creative production)	Create **digital artefacts** in a variety of forms and with attention to different users/ audiences.		
	Use digital tools to **gather and assess evidence**, make decisions and solve problems.		
	Take part in innovative **digital scholarship or professional practice**.		
Digital communication, collaboration and participation (participating)	**Communicate digitally** with others, including in public digital spaces.		
	Collaborate digitally, including with learners in other settings.		

Digital learning and development (development)	Develop **digital learning skills** and habits (eg note-making, referencing, tagging, curation, revision and review).		
	Support, mentor, coach or **develop others** with their digital skills, or use digital resources and tools to develop others.		
Digital identity and wellbeing (self-actualising)	Develop, manage and express their **digital identity**.		
	Consider their **digital safety**, **privacy**, **responsibility**, **health and wellbeing**.		

Appendix 2.1

Quick ILT Planner

1: Activity plan (learning content) • Question who, what, when, where, why and how? • Refer to the Display, Engage, Participation model (Chapter 3) to help with approach.	**2: Digital technology** • Select the digital technology that best supports the activity you intend to do. • Use your selected digital technology and see how well it works or not. • Summarise features, benefits and limitations of your choice of digital technology.

3: Learning activity (delivery) • What is your role during the use of the digital technology? • Use Bloom's Taxonomy to promote higher forms of thinking.	**4: Assessment (checking/ evidence)** • Assessment of and for learning.	**5: Resources** • List any useful resources, online links and materials to support learner's learning.

Appendix 3.1

Practical examples of using ILT

Acquisition/ assimilative	• Give audio feedback to learners. • Read and interact with content on a web page or an eBook. • Record and share audio files (podcasts) on social media sites. • Record coaching and mentoring sessions. • Record learner presentations or group work. • Record lecture or tutorial content for a flipped learning activity. • Record short 'talking head' videos. • Record short instructional video explaining a concept or introductory topic. • Record videos of learners carrying out practical activities for assessment. • Record your lecture and embed or upload to the VLE along with class notes and instructional questions. • Screencast feedback and annotations to learners on submission of work. • Screencast tutorial, narrating and giving a walkthrough of an online activity or resource. • Subscribe to online news feeds using a news aggregator as a means of keeping up to date with various websites or blogs. • Upload and share videos online through social media sites.
Discussion/ communicative	• Create a specific hashtag to enable learners to post and recall discussions, resources shared during an activity, lesson and conferences. • Create personal learning spaces for learners to learn independently internal and external to the classroom, both face-to-face and online. • Give feedback and suggest changes on an online collaborative document. • Host and facilitate a webinar, question and answer session, blended/distance-learning activities or tutorial with your learners. • Improve online communication and collaboration between you and learners by using social media sites, forums and chat rooms. • Post questions or topics online for learners to discuss and debate.

Investigative	• Collect and organise online resources that learners and colleagues find useful using online tools. • Create online surveys or questionnaires to check learning, obtain feedback or even allow learners to create their own and send to peers. • Mind-map and brainstorm ideas using online presentation tools. • Organise and store online documents and media on a cloud-based platform. • Set up an online glossary where learners can add their own definitions of words, phrases, acronyms or jargon. • Take notes using a mobile or desktop computer app. • Use internet search engines and social media sites to carry out specific searches or enquiries. • Use social bookmarking to organise useful websites and annotate over specific web page content. • Use social media to crowdsource information and use specific hashtags for the learning programme.
Practice/ experiential	• Allow 'bring your own device' (BYOD) so learners can assist and support themselves in their own learning. • Create a learning programme blog or allow learners to create their own to use as a reflective journal on what they have learned in a lesson or collectively over a period of time. • Create online tests and quizzes to check learners' learning and ease of marking. • Enable learners to obtain digital and open badges when they have completed a task or quiz in the VLE. • Enable manual completion or conditional release of activities in the VLE to encourage self-directed learning. • Encourage learners to create a professional identity using social networks like LinkedIn to connect with potential employers and industry experts. • Navigate through an online simulation that would otherwise be dangerous in the real world. For example, dealing with medical emergencies or learning virtual welding. • Promote online documents/post-it walls and IWB for active learning spaces.

Collaborative/ interactive	• Connect/synchronise your devices, platforms and systems (if necessary) to allow ease of access to view, collaborate and store digital content. • Create interactive annotated/hotspot images and videos. • Create, share and scan QR codes for interactive access to online resources and activities. • Enable learners to use their mobile devices to access teaching content you are displaying on the IWB. • Facilitate learning on an online document where learners can contribute and share resources. • Present learning content across tablets and/or learners' own devices for ease of interaction and participation. • Use augmented reality (AR) tools to layer the real world with digital content. • Use interactive polling so that learners can respond to questions or a debate (with their own mobile devices) – responses can be viewed live or for later assessment. • Use online project management tools to plan, work and learn in groups online and share outcomes. • Use the IWB to annotate over a PDF handout and invite learners to come up with and contribute knowledge and ideas to it – screenshot/screencast it and then upload to the programme's VLE. • Using a VLE in the classroom to access and participate in eLearning objects, such as introducing a concept for later discussion.
Productive	• Construct a knowledge base using a wiki, in which you can view a history of all changes. • Create and publish learning content as a website or an eBook. • Create, edit images and share them online on social media sites for use in learning and assessment activities. • Enable learners to create and share their own digital resources and publish as OERs for others to use and adapt. • Enable learners to set up a video channel and upload their recorded videos for assessment and comments from peers. • Upload project work, research or conference materials and share publicly. • Use online documents to type up assignments and share with tutors or other collaborators. • Use or enable learners to create their own ePortfolio for them to collect and present knowledge, skills and experience.

Appendix 3.2

Online activity readiness questionnaire

How likely are you on a scale of 1–5 to engage in the following kinds of online interaction? For example, in an online forum discussion (VLE), chat group (WhatsApp, www.whatsapp.com), social media (Twitter, https://twitter.com) etc.

What digital technologies are you confident in communicating with?						
Posting questions about your programme requirements, eg project work?						
Very likely	1	2	3	4	5	Very unlikely
Replying to others' posts when you know the answer?						
Very likely	1	2	3	4	5	Very unlikely
'Liking'/interacting with other learners' posts and comments?						
Very likely	1	2	3	4	5	Very unlikely
Posting your own thoughts about the learning programme?						
Very likely	1	2	3	4	5	Very unlikely

Replying to direct questions posted by your tutor?

Very likely	1	2	3	4	5	Very unlikely

Replying to other learners when they ask questions to the group?

Very likely	1	2	3	4	5	Very unlikely

'Positive silent engagement', engaging but not visibly contributing much or at all?

Very likely	1	2	3	4	5	Very unlikely

Posting links to resources that might be useful to other learners?

Very likely	1	2	3	4	5	Very unlikely

Posting a comment saying that you don't understand something so it will be repeated for you to get clarification?

Very likely	1	2	3	4	5	Very unlikely

Posting questions to encourage others to share their thoughts?

Very likely	1	2	3	4	5	Very unlikely

Posting to challenge other learners' ideas to stimulate discussion?

Very likely	1	2	3	4	5	Very unlikely

Reviewing a discussion to summarise what has been said on a topic?

Very likely	1	2	3	4	5	Very unlikely

Tagging your posts to make it easier to find or discover them?

Very likely	1	2	3	4	5	Very unlikely

Posting praising comments to other learners?

Very likely	1	2	3	4	5	Very unlikely

Posting thoughts on your struggles, challenges or anxieties about your learning?

Very likely	1	2	3	4	5	Very unlikely

Replying to others' posts to support those who have expressed struggles, challenges or anxieties with their learning?

Very likely	1	2	3	4	5	Very unlikely

Posting personal reflective experiences?

Very likely	1	2	3	4	5	Very unlikely

Posting 'off the cuff' topics to start discussions with other learners?

Very likely	1	2	3	4	5	Very unlikely

Displaying links on your profile that direct others to your personal sites?

Very likely	1	2	3	4	5	Very unlikely

Posting off-topic and responding to replies on these posts?

Very likely	1	2	3	4	5	Very unlikely

Appendix 6.1

Personal and professional development plan

Name:

Job role:

Period from:

Period to:

Development objective What knowledge or skills do I want to develop?	Development activity How will I achieve this? What is the most appropriate development activity?	What will I be doing differently? How will I know I have been successful? What key differences do you aim to make in your practice?	What do I not now need to do because of this change of approach? Identify what does not now need doing as a result of a new way of working. Don't take on extra work practices because nothing has been taken away.	Support needed? What resources or support will I need? Creative, technical, financial, time, resource.	Date for achievement Target dates for review/ completion.

Appendix 6.2

Learning log

Name:			Job role:	
Period from:			Period to:	
Date	What did you do?	Why?	What did you learn from this?	How have/ will you use this? Any further action?

Index